5 loaves
and 6 chicken nuggets

5 loaves, 2 fishes and 6 chicken nuggets

*Urinations from inside
the fast food tent*

Barry Gibbons

bright *i*s

First published in 2006 by
The Infinite Ideas Company Limited
36 St Giles
Oxford, OX1 3LD
United Kingdom
www.infideas.com

A CIP catalogue record for this book is available from the British Library

ISBN 10: 1-904902-88-X
ISBN 13: 978-1-904902-88-1

Designed and typeset by Sparks, Oxford – www.sparks.co.uk
Cover design by Cylinder, Suffolk
Printed in India

CONTENTS

INTRODUCTION

My interest in the combination of the words 'food' and 'quick' started at an early age. And I mean a very early age – probably within a few seconds of me taking my first breath. Let me explain.

I arrived on this planet dangerously ahead of schedule – many weeks premature. I've never seen any documentary evidence to confirm it, but apparently I weighed in at less than four pounds. Such was my condition, and the state of medical science at the time (1946), that I was not expected to see the night through. My response was not untypical of many I have given since when faced with one of life's mine-fields, namely to utter a rude word and then find something to eat. I slurped heartily during the night and, come the dawn, set off on my life's goal of putting on another 185 pounds.

My journey has, at times, represented a sort of dement-ed hopscotch. As a student, I had a variety of jobs to help with the funding. I worked in a pie factory, and saw things put in a pastry case that Saddam Hussein would have been reluctant to drop on the Kurds. I drove an ice-cream van, through Liverpool in the industrial north of England, with the external loudspeaker chime set at 78 rpm when it should have been 45 rpm. The locals reminisced that they had neither

seen nor heard anything like it since the Keystone Kops.
Later, I headed Bernie Inns, the UK's famous steakhouse
chain. In one memorable evening, between 6.00 p.m. and
10.45 p.m., I personally supervised one restaurant serving
385 meals on 100 covers. Most customers enjoyed their
meal, but some complained of dizziness.

This particular pilgrim's progress peaked when I was
handed responsibility for every Burger King on planet earth.
We were based on the coast in Florida, at the *exact* point
where some god had decreed that Hurricane Andrew would
come ashore in 1992, just three years after my arrival. I was
an Englishman running an American icon brand – and you
can imagine how the American franchisees took to me. To
this day, some of them celebrate my memory by sacrificing
a goat on my birthday.

I decided to quit 'big business' before my fiftieth birthday. It was my choice, and one not wholly celebrated by my
bank manager. I set off on a very different journey, splashing about in life's shallow end. My only goal was to forget
one person every day, so that when Alzheimer's eventually
arrived I would be ahead of the game.

Of course, it didn't work out like that. I ended up giving
speeches all over the world to vaguely interested business
audiences and writing books that consistently missed the
best-seller lists. I invested in businesses that had less going
for them than the pie inserts of the previous page.

And then, somehow or other, amidst all that, I agreed
to write some essays for a US magazine that is the clearing
house for all things to do with the quick-serve restaurant
business. This is an industry with which I was obviously
familiar, which popularly goes under the name of 'fast food'
and/or 'food service'. I repeated my successful formula from
previous years, which was to take a brief, study it diligently
– and then ignore it all together. Quick-serve food is not just
about five global US brands and not just about today. In one

form or another, it is worldwide and has been throughout history. If you step back from it, and look at it through a different pair of eyeglasses, you can conjure up some weird thoughts. Did the model for modern franchising (so loved in the quick-serve business) first see the light of day in the way Victorian England handed out chunks of India to loosely agreeing and agreeable princes? When, in history, was the first sandwich made – and of what and by whom? Can it be true that the world quick-serve's epicentre, *Place Jemaa el Fna*, in Marrakech, assembles itself from nothing, and then de-assembles itself again, all within the space of a few hours every evening? Is it possible to drive the few miles from the ruins of Pompeii to Sorrento, sit in the town square, and eat a quick-serve that is essentially the same as was being eaten by some poor guy when he was rudely interrupted by his own sudden death?

I am a man of iron discipline. My essays (nearly) always contained the words 'quick' and 'serve', but they increasingly reflected that particular business in the context of my fascination with history, geography and the issues facing a broader business church. And then something else happened.

The early 2000s saw a geometric increase in the number of people taking pot shots at the food industry in general, and quick-serves in particular. Some of them have been deserved because, on occasion, the industry seems to have a monopoly of daft people, ideas and practices. But it is also, in its widest sense, an enormous positive for the planet. It employs, creates wealth for, and feeds millions (and probably billions if you push the definition a bit) every day. It is hard to think of what the realistic alternative(s) might be.

So, while I was theorising about pre-neolithic flatbreads and business models from Crete, I also sought to provide some balance for the debate. Some famous military leader, whose name escapes me, was once asked why he sought a rather dubious party as an ally. His reply was succinct: 'I'd rather have him in my tent pissing out, than outside my tent pissing in.' These essays are posted from inside the industry tent.

It all resulted in approaching sixty essays, all of which have been rewritten for this book. They have been updated and (in some cases) embarrassingly rewritten as the passage of time occasionally threw doubts on my claim to have a monopoly of forecasting wisdom.

Welcome to this collection of *urinations from inside the fast-food tent*.

Barry Gibbons
Bedford, England, 2006

IN THE BEGINNING

The idea came at a rather inconvenient time, as most of mine do. Nowadays, I split my time between my UK home, which is near London, and Miami (which is near the United States), and my life is spent advising heads of state, Presidential candidates, and Chinese gangs. I was having a quiet one-on-one with Queen Elizabeth in a KFC in London – she likes food served in a cardboard bucket – and we were discussing my plan to grow Prince Charles's hair over the tops of his ears to stop him looking like a demented elephant calf, when her cellular phone rang out. It was for me. She was not amused.

It was the editor of a refined US journal, suggesting I write a series of essays on the quick-serve food business – 'fast food' to the uninitiated. As this is a subject that has fascinated me for nearly thirty years, I accepted on the spot. I was so happy I knocked over Her Majesty's bucket.

Serving food for a living is now one of the toughest challenges there is. Success in business is about achieving real distinction and generating widespread awareness in increasingly cluttered and competitive markets. Using that definition, quick-serve restaurants can make the case to be in the most cluttered and competitive market on the planet.

The good news is that the industry suffers less competition from the World Wide Web than most businesses involving a product or service sold to a customer. It's easy to sell a CD or book on the web, but tough to deliver a turkey sandwich in three minutes. The bad news is that that's really the end of the good news, because the industry goes about its difficult task with an almost Neanderthal mindset.

This is an industry that loves statistics – usually the wrong ones. During the five years of the First World War, about ten million people died untimely, awful deaths as a direct result of the conflict. About a million books have been written on the subject, and I bow to no one in the depth of my horror at the thought of it all. Immediately after the war, however, more than twice that many people died untimely and awful deaths from a new form of influenza – Spanish or Septic flu. Not as emotive, but in terms of the impact on the human race, profoundly more important. Even so, you'll have a job finding a book on it. In the same way, the foodservice industry loves statistics on 'cost of product' and 'same-store sales revenues'. I have never put either of those in the bank. The only thing that matters is sustainable cash flow. But that's like Spanish flu – you never hear about it.

Our SNAFUs are now legendary. Most of the industry is labour-intensive – unsurprisingly given that the middle letter in QSR stands for service – and a thousand gurus in ten thousand business books will tell you the key differentiator in a service business comes from the capability and motivation of the front-line people. So what do we do? We start them on minimum wage. And if we could start them on less, we would: correct? In London, it now costs about £6.00 an hour at a parking meter. If you work in a quick-serve there, you can look out of the window and see an iron pole earning more than you do. We usually train new employees by asking them to breathe on a mirror. If it fogs up, they're in there straight away, facing the customer, determining their experience. Annual labour turnover on the front line often exceeds 100 percent and sometimes three times that. If we tried, we couldn't do much more to alienate our troops. And then we leave our brands in their hands.

If sales are lower than planned, what do we do? We cut costs to defend earnings. Of course, if that's at the restaurant level, the only short-term (variable) costs to cut are those associated directly with the food, labour levels and maintenance – and indirectly with the advertising. So we respond to what is very likely a drop-off in the customer's perception of our market distinction, and/or their awareness of it, by worsening both of them. So, guess what? Revenues drop further. Now what can we do? Well, this time we'd better really reduce those variable costs …

Despite all this, the foodservice industry still fascinates us. Done correctly, it can still be the nearest thing to a theatre experience in the lives of millions of everyday folk. There are probably more smiles per day in the world's quick-serves than there are in the world's family homes. It has a special place in our hearts – after all, we know what goes on. Few people grow up without experiencing a spell working in a quick-serve. Those who do so are the worse for the omission. The pub in London, the noodle stall in Bangkok, the tapas bar in Madrid, and the infinite variety of quick-serves in the United States – they are all part of the host nation's fabric, which is probably why we tolerate stuff happening in them that would turn us homicidal in a shoe shop.

The Queen is excited by my new project, and asks me to pass on a message. If any of you reading this have an entry-level position open for a trainee, she has at least two names for you to consider. One has big ears.

IT'S ONLY ROCK 'N' ROLL

The history of the quick-service restaurant industry has an uncanny parallel with that of rock 'n' roll. Oh, I'm sure some form of quick-serves existed long before Bill Haley glued his kiss-curl into place and launched a hundred thousand cinema seat slashings; I'm sure somebody provided burgers for the Pony Express riders; and an adapted teepee probably dished up buffalo wings (literally) for Native Americans centuries before that. But the fact remains that when Ray Kroc was shaping the genesis of McDonald's, Elvis was howling his first attempts in the Sun studios for Sam Phillips. That's alright Mama.

I fell in love with both industries at around the same time. It wasn't always easy. On our new TV, my father watched as Jerry Lee Lewis sang 'Great Balls Of Fire' while playing the piano with his backside. Our TV was situated about three feet away from his collection of Rachmaninov records, which he played lovingly on a radiogram the size of a Land Rover. Thus we began a generation gap that eventually measured 2,309 linear miles in a house of about 1,750 square feet. We eventually narrowed it by me moving out.

I have watched both industries for half a century now. Surprisingly, rock music has some big lessons for quick service. Here are three to ponder.

If it's long-term success you want, the benefits of constant reinvention are widespread and obvious in rock. Almost the opposite is true in quick service. Take Eric Clapton. Every couple of years, his hairstyle changes, his eyeglasses change, his clothes and imagery change, his musical genre changes, at least slightly, and his musical 'allies' and backers change. *But it's still the same brand name, and the same core competence.* And it's still fresh and relevant after forty years in the world's most cluttered and competitive market. For Clapton, you could substitute McCartney, Paul Simon, Elton John, Madonna, or your own favourite rocker. Compare them with the big names in quick service – where all of them have faltered at one time or other, and had to scramble to try to recover. The lesson is in the adjective 'constant' fronting the word 'change'. Change even if you don't think it's needed.

Second lesson? It's the check and balance for the first one. Change isn't just about adding. You can get too complicated and confusing. Most rock groups were lean and mean, of necessity, in their early days. But as they stayed around and got richer, they became reliant on studio orchestras, huge concert productions, choruses of backing singers, multi-million-dollar videos, and so on. Winning competitiveness is about being distinct, and it became tough to pin down exactly what these guys were about. Then, when it threatened to get out of hand, realization set in. '*Unplugged*' saw them re-establish their basic distinction and offering, and many careers were salvaged.

In quick service, the lesson is clear. Change is needed, but don't just grow by adding products, complexity, and confusion. You try something new. Ditch something that's not working. Can you still perform unplugged? Don't let the world lose sight of why you were, and still are, good.

Finally, rock teaches this industry that if you can't perform live, you won't make it in the long term. If you look at any rock stars who have stayed the distance – some of them for forty-plus years now – they all have one thing in common: they can deliver, live, in concert. Sure, they have complemented this skill with studio technology and theatre, but the long-term winners, bar none, have always been able to deliver the goods on stage in front of an audience. It is very easy to look at the emperors of quick service and come up with ideas that might 'freshen' their offering, and draw more new and repeat customers, and heaven knows I am an advocate of trying out new things. But if these ideas are going to go beyond market testing – if they are going to become a part of the daily offering of the brand – you have to be able to deliver them consistently, in all geographies, at all times. They must be delivered on specification in the drive-through on a Monday night, and at 3.30 p.m. on a wet February afternoon. That's the 'big test' to put before the Chairman's new brainchild, or the new product development team's proposals. If you want to know how important this point is, buy yourself a ticket to a Rolling Stones concert – not to enjoy yourself, necessarily, but to understand the prime reason why they still fill venues and sell records more than forty years after I first saw them at the Apollo Theatre in Manchester, England. Does your brand deliver, to specification, every aspect of its act when you're home asleep?

Enough lessons. But I figured out long ago that nobody on the planet has a monopoly of wisdom, and the idea of being able to learn something from 'Keef' Richards appeals to some warped part of me. 'Keef' really is astonishing. I haven't seen anything as unwholesome looking since I once pondered the possibilities of eating a McRib.

Now, a competition: if the two industries are linked, what's the rock song title, from the past fifty years, best suited for a potential new quick-service brand? Email me at GibbonFile1@aol.com. We can only offer honour and publication as a prize. My entry is *Crying, Waiting, Hoping*, released by the Beatles in 1963.

TIME FOR REINVENTION 3

I am, of course, a definitive Boomer. I arrived at the ordering point of the drive-through of life in January 1946, the first full year of post-war peace. As it happens I arrived very early, weighed in at less than 4 lbs and was not expected to last the night. I survived, and immediately set about my life goal of putting on another 185 lbs.

Depending on which definition you use, I was followed by up to 100 million fellow-Boomers in the United States and Western Europe. From my deep research on the subject, I have one unchallenged observation about my peer group. We are all profound liars.

Here's an example. At the drop of a hat, or at the remotest hint of a lull in a conversation, a true Boomer will regale you with a reprise of his or her exploits from the 1960s – which has to be a lie. If they were Boomers, they wouldn't remember what happened in the sixties. Take my story, for instance. There were four of us who were inseparable friends: me, Ernesto 'Che' Guevara, Bob Dylan and Cassius Clay. We went everywhere together, and, my, oh my, did we get into some scrapes. One night, in the mid-sixties, just before the Newport Folk Festival, I remember we were crowded into Bob's dressing room. We were all working with him on the lyrics to *Maggie's Farm* when he suddenly looked up and told us he was going to forsake his folk-singing heritage and go 'electric'. We told him he was mad. He had just achieved icon status as the legitimate heir to Woody Guthrie, and here he was throwing it all away.

As if that wasn't enough, Cassius soon turned his back on everything that had secured his champion status – renouncing his name, religion and the establishment that had promoted him. He then re-emerged as Muhammad Ali, which seemed to us another daft idea doomed to failure.

What history shows is that neither of them threw anything away. They both looked at their level of achieved success, and – for whatever reasons – decided to change. In their case, however, change wasn't about tweaking. It was a fundamental reinvention of everything they did and stood for. At the time, it wasn't seen to be risky – it was seen to be suicidal, because nobody else saw the need for it. Everybody forecasted doom.

What happened, of course, was the opposite. In both cases, they took themselves to higher levels, actually grew the markets they operated in, and became global statesmen.

Let's contrast their brave approach to change with the quick-serve restaurant industry generally, and some of its 'stars' specifically. For sure, there have been substantive changes. (And, equally for sure, still more are needed.) If you look at any of the great names of today, they bear little or no resemblance to their genesis models in the 1950s. There has been huge and fundamental change.

So, what's the problem? The problem was – and remains – in the timing and mental approach to change in this business. Almost every substantive change in the quick-service industry came as a response to a period of worsening performance. It came after a peak of success. It came when owners, investors, franchisees and customers (delete as applicable) were becoming increasingly unhappy with what they were getting out of the current offering. It came from increasing pressure to do something – almost anything – to stop a down-trend. It was reactive to decline, not proactive to new growth opportunities. I do not believe the history of the quick-service industry has witnessed one Dylan-esque or Ali-esque example of reinvention before everybody else saw the need for it. The movers and shakers in quick service do not have the mindset to take risks with what seems a successful concept, one that seems to have some mileage left in it. The strategic approach to change falls somewhere between 'If it ain't broke, don't fix it' and 'Milk it for every penny, then we'll figure out what comes next'.

Does it matter? After all, we can cheerfully agree that 'big changes' have happened over the period in question, so what's the big deal? I think it does matter. Reactive change is usually just a sticking plaster. It addresses the symptom, not the disease. The whole mentality of change management in this scenario is one of doing as little as possible to get by; to prop the figures up again for a few quarters. Then you repeat the whole thing – probably with a new executive team and advertising agency. Proactive reinvention is different. It is enormously risky, and you are constantly ambushed by the CW2 guys ('It Can't Work, Won't Work').

But you are thinking ahead positively, not backward negatively. You are planning your growth with a clear mind. You are also planning to change and grow the actual market within which you operate. And you are planning for long-term success – to be a market icon or statesman.

The quick-service world is now made up of brands and operations with sticking plasters all over them. How significant is that? If somebody had thought like Dylan or Ali, *one of the 'Big QSR Names' would have invented Starbucks.*

Now, did I tell you about the four of us and the Cuban Missile Crisis? How I won £10 in this crazy bet with Che Guevara? Man, those were the days …

ONLY THE GOOD DIE YOUNG

Those who are familiar with my entry in *Who's Who* often remark on the things I have omitted. For rather obvious reasons, I have deliberately left out my gold medals from the Berlin Olympics, my 'friendship' with Tallulah Bankhead, and the fact that I am the last First World War fighter-pilot ace writing about fast food.

A rather more surprising omission, however, is my Nobel Prize for QSRs, awarded in the early 1990s. It was awarded, if you remember, for my breakthrough work on the genome of Burger King's Chicken Tenders. Yes, it was I who finally solved the mystery of the DNA architecture of this astonishing product.

The linking of scientific thesis and fast food has been frequent, and, in my observation, almost always useless. In my time, I have personally been confronted by thousands of pieces of scholarship on the subject and ignored them all.

Bouncing around the internet recently was a piece by Carol Sorgen, a distinguished medical writer. With umpteen quotes, and references to other people's works (all of whom had letters after their names), a thesis was advanced that suggested fast food can be healthy. It seems possible to have a low-fat meal in a quick-serve, and also possible to have a meal that has a good supply of nutrients. The bad news is, and I quote, 'It's going to take some planning'.

Just what we need. Welcome to the future. Going to a KFC is to become like D-Day.

I have nothing against Ms. Sorgen, and wish her well. Fortunately, the Constitution allows me to say that I found the piece to be the most vacuous and pointless treatise I've come across in years. And, remember, I've seen Sting live in concert.

There are only two attitudes to fast food: acceptance and non-acceptance. Those who harbour the latter disposition would not go in a quick-serve to save the lives of children. So, there is no point writing anything with them in mind. Interestingly, those who accept it may not actually frequent quick-serves, but the important point is that they accept that quick-serves play many roles in the lives of millions of people. Those roles may range from the provision of an essentially cheap substantial meal each day, to the provision of what many people openly prefer to a gourmet meal of pan-fried pigeon breasts nestling on a bed of wilted spinach.

In all the roles the quick-serves play to this audience, it is my observation that affecting health by a marginal amount by skipping this or downsizing that is never present. The arrival of more choices – both for eating in and eating out – plus the wider understanding of broad health issues, has already happened. But that's like off-stage music. Quick-serve users have made their minds up at another place and time as to what role quick-serves play in their lives, so how about just having faith in them to use their own best judgement?

I do know this: if the providers of quick-serves think users will be influenced by quick-service-specific health sermons, they are making a big mistake. Almost every effort I have seen that aspires to the changing of behaviour in quick service for 'health' reasons has failed. It doesn't matter if it was the provision of a special 'healthy' product, advertising, information, or even changing a brand name – it tanked.

In the early 1990s, we in Burger King tested a (relatively!) healthy version of the Whopper, along with countless other 'healthy' new products. None of the 'healthy' stuff tested well enough to launch (particularly if it was marketed as 'healthy'), but it was the reaction to the idea of altering the make-up of the Whopper that astonished me. To mis-quote Tom Clancy – the clear and present message we got back from test markets was: 'Do not, under any circumstances, mess with the Whopper. We may only eat one a week, or even one a year. But when we do, we want it to dribble down our chins during eating. And we insist that the calorific intake associated with eating it, together with fries, ketchup and a soda, remains the equivalent of that eaten by the total population of Pakistan during an average week. And if you do change it, buddy, you will be in big need of the Federal Witness Protection Program.'

Health, and healthy eating, are not complicated. They do not need science, lectures, sermons, or nannying. Quickserves have played a part in my life – as has every other kind of eat-in and eat-out experience. What is needed is a personal philosophy and some life rules. My waist was 34″ (that's 86 cm to you metricated types) in 1965 and has been the same ever since. Follow these rules and never worry about your health, your food, or where you eat again:

- Never eat anything you can't lift.
- Never eat anything that has any green in it.
- Never eat anything described as 'tasting like chicken'. (This rule is particularly important in South Korea.)
- Never eat anything that doesn't have lungs.
- Never eat anything that is surrounded by dead flies.
- Most important – never eat anything that has to be explained by a waiter.

IN DEFENCE

L ike most writers operating in the world of food and beverages, I have my sources in the Vatican. A few weeks ago, two of them e-mailed me with a 'heads-up' warning on a terrifying pending announcement. In a panic I rushed to Italy, but my personal plea remained unheeded. A senior theologian of the Catholic Church issued a statement condemning the quick-service food industry. I quote the translated version of his historic epistle: 'The sense of community is absent, fast food is not a model for Catholics.'

Now, I don't want to get off on a Grumpy Old Men-style rant here. And I should declare, at the outset, that I am not religious in the normal sense. I am a Paranoid Agnostic, not believing in a God as such, but believing there is a force out there that is out to get me. My thoughts on Catholicism, specifically, are those of anybody with a healthy mind on a religious Establishment that has only just ratified Copernicus' work and is still uneasy with Darwin. But in this case I am going to let fly – this guy is dead wrong.

This attack essentially bemoans the death of the collective meal, which has been one of history's binding agents for the family. The traditional family model – with its associated behaviour, activities and attitudes – has all but gone, and

I share the sadness at its passing. But to put a chunk of the blame on fast food is fatuous. The biggest single element in the deconstruction of the family came when Mum stopped shouting 'C'mon guys, dinner's ready, come and get it' and moved to 'Hey Billy (or Mary), whaddya want to eat? Can I ding something in the microwave for you? Then you can eat it while phoning your friends, and somebody else will clean up afterwards.' I look forward to a Catholic edict on the effects of this change of behaviour on the family, and, while we are at it, on TVs in kids' bedrooms, anti-social behaviour orders, iPods, working mothers and mobile phones.

The age we live in has thrown massive change at all of us. Some of it is phenomenally good, but most of that is accompanied by stuff we can't handle. Unprecedented wealth creation has benefited millions – but it has been divisive, with the gap between rich and poor widening. There are still too many poor people in rich countries, and too many rich people in poor ones. The 'information age' has revolutionised every aspect of accessing data and communication – but opened cyberspace to bomb makers, identity thieves and sexual predators. These are the uncomfortable by-products of progress, as is the demise of the 'traditional' family.

I am sick of the quick-service world taking hits from shallow thinkers who can't see beyond the end of their quills. Everybody has a go – QSRs are air-dirtiers, carcinogen generators, body-fat developers, and now, it seems, family destroyers. Let me give the detractors a couple of fast foods for thought.

If you go into a McDonald's in any shopping mall on a Saturday, at lunchtime, you will see families eating together – some of them (I grant you, not all of them) happily smiling and chatting amongst themselves. If you examine the whole postal code that contains that mall, during the same lunch hour, you will not find a single family together at a domestic table. Trust me.

When I was CEO of Burger King, I used to get millions of figures shovelled in front of me. One stuck in my mind then and is still with me today. We sold two million Whoppers every day across the world. That's two million people – about 0.035% of the earth's total population – who got at least one cheap, hot, substantial, nourishing meal in every twenty-four-hour period. And here's another aspect that these gloomy plonkers find hard to handle: Most of these two million who opt for the Whopper, or whatever else it might be from the huge range of fast food available, do so because they prefer it.

Is fast food destroying the health of the civilised world? This probably annoys me most of all. Of course, if you eat three large pizzas a day, seven days a week, for thirty years, you will explode, Monty Python-style, and discolour several nearby walls. Ditto hamburgers, fried chicken, burritos, fish and chips, kebabs, chicken jalfrezi and anything else – quick, slow, or self-service. But quick-service restaurants are not the problem here. Personal weakness and/or addiction and/or greed are the problems. It becomes a matter of how you use the quick-serve and how you eat.

I loved Julia Child, the (sadly now deceased) American Earth Mother of cooking. She talked more common sense than any hundred of the current TV chef-entertainers. Listen to what she says about how to eat: 'Small helpings, no seconds, no snacking, a little bit of everything, and have a good time.' It is my observation (although sadly not my personal experience) that if you applied such glorious common sense to any way of eating, you would be perfectly healthy. If you applied it to a life and a diet that had to be, or was by choice, predominantly in quick-service restaurants, you would be just fine.

Now I must rush. My sources in Tibet have just informed me that His Holiness, the new Dalai Lama, is going on prime time TV to complain about the American habit of putting cheese in cans. This I might find tough to defend.

CRUMBUG:
A CALL FOR ACTION

Normally, my inventions crash and burn on take off. This might have something to do with the marks I scored in my last science exams in 1962. I got 3% in chemistry and 4% in physics. Or it may have been the other way around. Hence, when I went to the market with my breakthrough electric snooker cue some years later, the market took no notice.

I have, however, invented a language. Well, not the language itself, but the name for a language that is now widely spoken and written.

I arrived at Burger King more than ten years ago. The company, which was then part of the Pillsbury group, had become the 'victim' of one of the last contested corporate acquisitions of the second millennium. The 'victor' company was then called GrandMet. I worked for them in London, and I either won or lost some straw-drawing competition (I've never been sure which) and arrived at BK's corporate headquarters in Miami as soon as the ink had dried on the deal.

Contested acquisitions usually get ugly. The defending company's shareholders are normally happy, but the defending management team normally fight to the death with everything and anything. This usually includes character assassinations of the predatory company's management.

This whole process involves assembling stuff that might prove embarrassing when you lose, and the new management team arrives.

This explains why, when I arrived and found my way to my new office (in which you could have held a small Cup Final) the drawers were empty. There wasn't a document anywhere – with one exception. Looking forlorn and lonely, the Pillsbury Mission and Values Statement was in a frame hanging on the wall. As I read it, two things occurred to me. The first was the irony. If the company had lived by half of the articulated contents, I would never have been there reading it – Pillsbury would never have fallen in combat. This was a real tension breaker, and I finished reading it with a big grin on my face.

The second point was one of style. Have you ever read one of these things? They are full of split infinitives ('to boldly go …'). There are at least six adverbs per column inch. Tonally, they are arrogant and out of touch with reality. This particular one was so full of crap and humbug that, there and then, I invented my new language name: *Crumbug*.

Go and read your company's statement. Look at those of other companies (somebody has put a collection of them in a book). If you can come up with a better name for the language, I will cede the floor to you. I know a bunch of top executives – and many of them spend hours, days, weeks, word-smithing Crumbug. In their judgement it is vital that an assortment of corporate audiences, internal and external, understand the common goals and values of the organisation. That may be true, but if it is, writing Crumbug is not a good use of a leader's time. It is a good use of a hired-in English professor's time. A leader's job is to have a dream: to see future shapes that others don't see – shapes that will give the company winning distinction. The leader shouldn't try to articulate these shapes – they are best if they can be drawn in crayon. In the dreary world of 1950s clothing retailing, Luciano Benetton saw a different kind of clothes shop. He saw a shape that changed retailing forever. I suspect he never wrote it down.

The leader then delegates to deliver the dream. You find the best people with the best skills you can. The leader should keep refining the dream. The minute it is articulated, it is out of date. Five paragraphs of mission-specific Crumbug, framed and hung on the cafeteria restroom wall, is my idea of a suicide note.

Of course, the leader has a wider role than to sit alone with a box of crayons. But that role moves away from what the company does, to how the company does it. It is through the leadership that we get a read on the character of the company. We see its personality, and find out what it stands for. Yes, these are its values. But these are not things you write down in Crumbug. These are things that people who work in or with the company see and hear every day. When a company treats a long-standing supplier like dirt – bingo, there's a value for all to see. When a company fires a twenty-year veteran employee by e-mail, hey, guess what – there's another one. If a company allows a management Hitler to rule a department by fear, it tells you all you need to know. If you can't get a response to a customer query, ditto. *Values aren't things you write down, they are things you do* – good and bad, all of you, in the company, every day. They are not things you read – they are self-evident. Other people tell you what your values are.

Now, I must boldly go. I am writing this on a plane. My values are such that, at all times, I will be an equal-opportunity, non-discriminatory air traveller. I will fairly treat all fellow passengers with courtesy and sensitivity. But if this fat geezer doesn't stop banging his lard-arse into me while he stuffs his oversize carry-on bag into the overhead compartment that *already contains mine*, I will pull his pants down. You may frame that and put it on your cafeteria wall.

YOU CAN'T FLY SOLO

I split my life between bases in an English village near London and a place in Miami (Cuba's northernmost suburb). Let me bring you some news from England's bustling capital.

Drinkers are intrigued by the fact that a beer that cost the publican the equivalent of less than fifty pence now costs more than three pounds across the bar. Shoppers in the supermarket are getting used to the fact that you can quite easily get seventy-five pounds' worth of groceries in one of those check-out bags. Female executives in the city are alarmed by the arrival of a high-profile American (female) executive who is attended twice during her office day by her beautician. All strange stuff – but nothing has confused us more than McDonald's buying stakes in other (small) food-service outfits.

None of the big players in the quick-service industry flies completely solo – that is, owns and manages everything it does. It is not possible. But alliances and partnerships within the industry make for an interesting study. So, you want to be a millionaire? Here's your first question for £100. In Burger King, if you buy a cola, you buy Coca-Cola. What, in your opinion, should be the brand name on the paper cup you drink it out of? Should it be:

(a) Coca-Cola?
(b) Burger King?
(c) Plain, white, unbranded?
(d) The latest promotional offer?

It is, of course, mostly 'b', and occasionally 'b' mixed with 'd'. However, I am quite clear: it should always be 'a'. My reasons? I was behind Burger King's switch from Pepsi to Coke in the early 1990s. They are both fine liquids, particularly if you have any jewellery that needs cleaning and, penny for penny, there was not much difference in the cost. Coke pitched as partners; Pepsi pitched as suppliers. Now, if BK is selling a cola that prides itself in being one of the world's great drink brands, why the hell wouldn't it say so on the cup? It also, rather pragmatically, occurs to me that the place the public sees these cups most is in the street gutter, where their presence is extremely negative. Another good reason to keep BK off it.

Partnerships are of all shapes and sizes. They may be about high-profile co-branding, like BK and Coke. They may be about a vendor/supply-chain relationship – for example, the provision of produce. It may be a banking or financing partnership. It may be with an advertising agency. It may be about diversification, like McDonald's seems to be signalling with its growing number of interests in roast chicken, gourmet sandwiches, Mexican food, and specialty coffee – a case of putting some fresh eggs in a (big) basket of mature ones.

There are infinite types of partnership, but to succeed they must have one thing in common. They must work for both sides. They must be win–win. As the Chinese proverb says, a good agreement is where both sides leave the table smiling. It is this aspect that bothers me about this growing practice. It's not the usual Western way of doing business. The Western way is about winning, and gaining at somebody else's expense.

Legend has it that if you send a group of Western (male) executives to a business school and get them together in the bar after a long day, you can play a simple, entertaining game. Pick two guys, and make a mark on the floor between them. Tell each of them to try to convince the other, verbally, to come across the line. The results are astonishing. They will still be there next morning. Now, if you do the same thing in Japan, within five minutes the two guys will have an agreement. One will say to the other: 'I'll come over to your side if you'll come over to mine'. There is no winner. Or loser.

If you spend hours at your office, huddled with your lawyers, trying to find ways to screw your partner, it is not a partnership. It is a practice that will rule out a sustainable, healthy win–win relationship. Contrast two examples. For years, Ray Kroc had a handshake deal with many of his major suppliers. Included in those years are those where McDonald's broke away from the pack and made itself the quick-service brand of the millennium.

Now look at those fatheads in DaimlerChrysler. A while back they hit an earnings shortfall. In a moment of lunacy that only a German management team operating in the United States could come up with, they announced that all their suppliers would cut wholesale prices by 5%. No debate, no consideration of individual circumstances. Result? Chaos. Some suppliers refused to deliver and a red-faced climbdown followed. More important, partners who might have proved allies in a common cause were now enemies. A bank of goodwill was emptied at a stroke. A potential solution became another problem.

As in life, so it is in quick service. You cannot fly solo. Partnerships work, but they need working on. Just think: if Burger King did make its own brand of cola, what would it be like? It might be like its coffee. An ugly, ugly thought.

EVEN THE BIG CHEESE
MUST BUDGET

What happens in America usually takes two or three years to reach England. As a Brit, it was, therefore, with a feeling of horror that I saw my first US-style stretch limo over here. It was parked in front of a four-hundred-year-old village pub, and looked like a cold sore on the face of Elizabeth Hurley. The stretch limo is universally associated with Hollywood and/or rappers and/or the trappings of corporate power in the United States, and I need to start by revealing my views on limos. Yes, I confess I have been inside several of them, but my ongoing position is that I would not willingly go in one today, even if it offered me the only escape route from a pack of wild dogs snapping at my genitals.

More than a decade ago, as a newly appointed – and imported – CEO of Burger King, I inherited a wonderful assistant. She assumed that the new boss would be the same as the old boss and booked a limo to pick me up as I arrived at Orlando airport on an early head-hunting mission. Knowing no different, I got in the thing, which then proceeded *about a hundred yards* to the airport hotel where the meeting was scheduled. I could have got in the back, walked *through the car*, got out of the front door and had my meeting. I banned them for all corporate use.

A couple of years later, we booked 'Stormin' Norman' Schwarzkopf to speak at our annual convention. At the hotel, we were all on standby to receive the great man, with a bunch of secret service guys hanging about, their eyes never still. The walkie-talkies suddenly crackled and up pulled a huge limo. The door opened, and out stepped my tiny wife. The hotel had sent this doozie to pick her up at the airport. She, not knowing any different, had got in. As everybody stared silently at her getting out, some of them wondering if they should shoot her, Norman pulled up behind – in an old red pick-up truck.

There and then I formed SEAL (Senior Executives Against Limos) and I have remained president, treasurer, and the only paid-up member ever since. It begs the question, of course, as to what is the correct degree of ostentation you should enjoy as a 'big cheese'. There are negatives to a fully egalitarian approach – I remember one of my corporate managers pleading with me to be a bit more flash when I visited franchisees. His message was that they expect ostentation from a corporate leader, that they want their employees and their competitive peers to see that they belong to a system of substance, and that they are led by a Big Time Charlie. The point is also made, of course, that if you are in the junior ranks of a company, labouring away for 24/7 in an office the size of Fatty Arbuckle's coffin, if you don't believe there is a big office and a load of perks at the end of your rainbow, there is not much to keep you turning up and motivated. Each to his (or her) own.

There is, however, a clear trend towards reducing the excesses of corporate style invoked by business leaders, if for no other reason than it can tick off the Stock Exchange and/or investors and/or pressurised employees by giving off the wrong kind of signals. I have stopped judging all this by car length or office square-footage. There is an appropriate level of cost necessary to support the effectiveness and efficiency of each job in a corporation. Corporate cost is like the fresh water barrel on a fifteenth-century galleon crossing the Atlantic. The water has to get everybody there alive. It's finite, and there's not much of it. If one person uses more, another must use less. If it runs out, everybody dies. It calls for judgement.

This approach can justify the private jet – but only if it is used like Sam Walton used it. His life was visiting Wal-Marts, day in day out, all over America. He was frugal in the extreme with normal overhead costs, but everybody agreed he added real value visiting stores. A private plane probably doubled or trebled his annual store visit tally and was money well spent.

On the other hand, this approach can't justify a limo if it's only about image and pampering. One of my old bosses was driven, in a stretch limo, on his own, from home to work and back every day. It was such an important part of his image that he had a structural wall knocked out in the under-office car park to cater for his big sardine tin.

Both stories tell you all you need to know about right and wrong in this game. Spend what you need to spend to support your job description. No less, no more. That's a ruling that should apply to every job. If you are sending a junior manager to Japan, give them a first-class air ticket. If they are important enough to represent you, the cost of getting them there fresh is justified. Conversely, if you are a big cheese and you are hopping a short distance, shock everybody and drive yourself or fly economy. Your lifestyle is determined by your salary and how you spend it, not corporate perks.

I fear the only way I will stop this unwanted limo invasion in England is to start a scare. So, if you read of an outbreak of mad-limo disease in the UK sometime soon, and read of the government slaughtering them all, you can smile quietly to yourself. And you can still apply to join SEAL.

THE GIANTS'
CHANGING FACES

I am in Turin, at a convention of European shopping-mall developers. They have just realised that the provision of food and drink at such facilities is er ... er ... well, helpful to all concerned. While we are in the old city, we grab a look at the famous Shroud (or, at least, a life-sized replica). Everybody has his or her own theories as to its origin and whether it is fake or real. So have I – it looks like a prank played by one of the Bee Gees in the 1970s after a heavy post-concert party. One of them covered himself in treacle and fell asleep.

With my limited Italian, I try to read *La Stampa*, the local newspaper. Suddenly I find myself trembling, with a dreadful constriction in my throat. Unless my translation is way off, just over the Alps and across the border in Switzerland, the first McDonald's hotel has opened. One picture tells me everything I can't translate – the headboards on the beds in the double rooms are shaped like golden arches. The only restaurant in the hotel is a McDonald's. This is Switzerland, remember: a tiny country with France and Italy as neighbours – nations responsible for two of the planet's great culinary cultures. It gets worse. I think I translate the last sentences of the article correctly: *McDonald's is targeting business travellers.*

Now then, should this earth ever require a stereotypical business traveller to send to an inter-planetary business travelling convention, it would be me. I have spent much of my adult life in planes and hotels. I have visited more than thirty countries on business. They are, therefore, and by definition, targeting me. So, let me tell you what they are up against. Should I be lucky enough to have a business visit to Switzerland, and my searches on the web tell me that there are 6,512 hotel options, a McDonald's hotel would not even be my 6,512th choice. No, sir. If all the other 6,511 were full, I would book a room in Northern Italy, get up early, and walk (if there was no elephant to hand) across the Alps to my meeting.

Are they mad? The answer, I suspect, is *no*. There are some odd bits and pieces going on in McDonald's, which, if you look at them as a whole, suggest something quite revolutionary might be going on. It might also be a quick-service industry first. By any measurement, McDonald's is one of the world's great brands. The science of branding has changed irrevocably in the past decade, and my observation is that we are seeing the first of the quick-serve giants recognizing this.

For the last century or so, branding has been about products. Coca-Cola is the classical exponent of this approach – and Mars, Ford and Heinz are but three of many other examples. Branding is about differentiation – distinction – in cluttered and competitive markets. What has changed is how you get that distinction effectively and efficiently. Much less emphasis is being placed on *what* you do (the specification and price of your product or service). What's winning and retaining business today is *how* you go about delivering that to the market. What you do still matters, of course, but it is the price of entering the game. To win it, you must add style to substance. What you stand for as a business, and the company's 'personality', are becoming critical differentiators. Branding by reputation, not product, is the name of the new game.

I cannot think of one product that could sustain a mighty corporation today, let alone give it a platform to grow. Coca-Cola led the way in the cola wars throughout the 1990s, but has now been overhauled by Pepsi. If you look at Pepsi's armoury of drink products today, many of which are (gasp!) non-carbonated, you will see a very different approach to brand ownership and management evolving.

Now let's go back to McDonald's. It was forever associated with a one-dimensional product and corporate personality. Now look what's happening. The company is into gourmet coffee, and has signalled it is targeting one of the spiritual homes of espresso coffee – Austria – to develop this potential growth sector. McDonald's is duelling with the French, adapting its traditional menu to reflect that when the outlets are in Paris, they are not in Wyoming. It has also acquired Mexican and rotisserie chicken foodservice businesses.

Do I see Coke and Pepsi and Macs getting into the dumb stuff of the past two decades and buying film studios? Short answer: no. But they are changing their faces. They are moving away from single-product dependence – not because those products have no life left in them, but because they are too limiting in *personality* and growth potential.

The only limit here is your imagination. The Swiss Army, which doesn't actually fight, is famous for its penknives and watches. It will shortly (or so I've heard) launch a range of *lingerie*, which will be followed by the Swiss Army chocolate range, and then the Swiss Army Wine Club.

There is a new future for you out there if you can just open your mind.

NO WONDER WE ARE
LIVING LONGER

I am floating on the Mediterranean, face up, feet towards France. I am determined to do two things, both of which require superhuman determination. First, I will keep my toes above water until further notice. Second, I will write this chapter (in principle, you understand, even I cannot float with a laptop).

I am inspired by a recent *Provençale* luncheon, which started promptly at 1.00 p.m. under the olive trees of our rented farmhouse and which finished, in delightful disorganisation, the whole thing not aided by beakers of Calvados, around midnight.

My theme will be a short, two-dimensional history of executive dining, culminating in my observations about the correct eating habits for the modern businessperson. I say two-dimensional because it will be based on my personal experiences, and they span both a long passage of time, and a business career that hopped from Europe to America. Both dimensions need analysis before the conclusion.

In my early days, back in England, an executive would not dream of starting the day's labours without the Full Monty breakfast. Nor would he (and in those days it was about 99% male) contemplate eating this anywhere but in his own (domestic) dining room. Such a breakfast had a number of requirements. First, it would need two butlers, a chef, probably a *sous* chef, and three kitchen maids. Second, all dishes would be served from under the lids of silver platters lined up on a table by a roaring fire (even in summer). Third, there would have to be at least three dishes beginning with 'k' (kippers, kidneys, kedgeree, etc.). Work-talk was forbidden; phone calls were unheard of. Our man read *The Times*, which had probably been ironed by a third butler. Somewhere around 9.30 a.m., fully bolstered for the trials ahead, he would head towards the train station, drift into London and float into the office.

Luncheon was the meal for business – and notice it is luncheon, not lunch. This was not a rushed affair, and due process was rigorously observed on a number of fronts. The venue had to be away from prying eyes, preferably a private club where occasional indiscretions were gently rubbed with vanishing cream. It would start around 1.00 p.m., *and no business was discussed before 4.00 p.m.* Then, it was all concluded quickly, hands were shaken, and God help anybody who went back on his word. Luncheon was also the first proving ground of an astonishing mathematical phenomenon: half a bottle of wine is perfect for one, but a full bottle is not quite enough for two.

The late afternoon saw the dictation of a letter or two back at the office, with the frugal accompaniment only of hot tea and a selection of cakes. Cocktails began promptly at 7.30 p.m., and a curtain came down – no more business affairs would be aired through that or dinner.

The 'Big Bang' changed it all. That was when London went all high-tech and 24/7. The equivalent executive today has a breakfast of wheatgerm extract while running on a treadmill, sending and receiving e-mails on something called a BlackBerry, swallowing vitamins and watching his – or her – Bloomberg screen. And it is still only 5.00 a.m. Said executive may not eat again until late evening, when he/she regroups with a bunch of stressed-out peers around an organic (and team-bonding) vegetarian pizza. Caffeine is forbidden after 11.30 a.m., and the idea of wine with anything would send our hero/heroine into a three-month course of counselling.

Somewhere in this transition, I moved to America – and a whole new set of variables was introduced to my confused digestive system. In 1990, having just arrived in the United States, I sat opposite a young (male) executive in a New York deli. The time was about 11.00 a.m. – neither one thing nor the other. He ordered a chopped liver sandwich. It arrived, and it was about six inches thick. To my dying day I will never forget the horror of him eating it across the table from me. Slowly, like a reticulated python, he unhinged his lower jaw, and swallowed it whole. I swear I could see the whole shape of it as it headed down his gullet.

The changing habits of business eating have happened in the States in parallel with Europe, but our analysis of them must factor in two unique-to-Uncle-Sam elements, namely size and speed. Rule Number One is that good equals big, and a well-received meal in the US is still one you can't see over. To this day, I have nightmares about the amount of food ordered and left uneaten.

Speed is the other unique factor (that is, speed as in quick service). In Europe, it can take one hundred years to get a garden lawn to its first stage of acceptability. A game of cricket between two countries can take five days, during which the players stop for lunch and tea each day. England now boasts an official 'Slow Food' movement. We like things slow.

Sadly, however, nowadays we are all much the same in our executive lives and habits. True, the Italians and French have defended a proper lunch, but most of us have changed with the demands of the times, and most of us are influenced by American-led habits and brands such as Starbucks.

Today, my breakfast is All Bran, and skimmed milk. I don't do luncheon – I eat lunch or brunch, and have no alcohol. But now and again, the rebel in me rears up and I clear the decks for the afternoon and evening, and get tucked in. I hit Joe Allen's at 1.00 p.m., and head for my train about 5.30 p.m., frequently getting lost on the way back to the station. I attempt to read London's evening paper, until I realise that it is upside down and give up the ghost. Sure, I pay for it the morning after, but I can see from here you are all jealous.

And that's not all I can see. My toes have disappeared. I must head for land.

11

TAKING TO THE STREETS

The plan is working all right, but I am paying a personal price.

As you know (and I'd like you to keep it to yourselves as much as possible), for some years now I have enjoyed a not-insubstantial monthly retainer, which has been paid into my Swiss bank account on behalf of one of the more notorious Chinese gangs.

The plan is to undermine most, if not all, Western governments and their lackey 'global' brands, so that, when the Great Day arrives, they will have been weakened and will be capable of less resistance. I have been recording notable success. As I said, however, I am paying a price. I made my mark on all the recent summit meetings of the G8 and the heads of Western democracies, and so far I have totted up a broken leg, five broken ribs, and pepper-spray burns (Seattle); a cracked skull, one lost eye, and nine broken fingers (Scotland); and I am still recovering from the bruising and the rubber-bullet wounds that the Genoa police handed me. These G8 meeting are getting tougher every year. There may have been some damage to my liver from the Edinburgh escapade, but, in fairness, that might have been due to the sixty-two single malts that I had before I took to the streets for my peaceful protest.

I disguised my true cause well, hiding under the umbrella of (at various times) the following 'campaigns': anti-globalisation; pro-Kyoto; anti-whaling; anti-salmon farming; anti-genetically modified crops; anti-capital punishment; pro-cannabis legalisation; Save The Tiger; Don't Save McDonald's; ban pesticides; Minimum Wage For Nike Slaves; Third-World debt relief; Shoot Charlton Heston; and Bring Back Abba.

Just what is it these Western leaders don't get? Just because I have a job, money in the bank, a family, two cars, three pensions and all the toys I could wish for, can't they understand I am still angry? There is a fire burning within me, and I need to trash buildings and throw Molotov cocktails at fascist-pig policemen to make my point.

Now then, let's you and me stop and reflect a moment. Does anybody know what the hell is going on here? No citizen of a developed nation should fail to understand that there is something different happening on the streets. As I write, France seems to be being burned down city by city (or, at least, car by car). It is ugly, by our own conventional definitions, but it is still some distance away from affecting our daily lives. There is a chance it never will – unless we live in a city daft enough to host a summit. As yet, I suspect it has not influenced big business decisions, other than at the margin. But it might soon encompass both, and we should therefore seek to understand it.

I lived through the industrial relations 'wars' in British business, which was bad enough. I have witnessed firsthand the fight against racism, and other forms of discrimination, in the United States – but never have I seen two 'sides' so distant in core values. The big governments and global corporations spout righteous objectivity – that we must have law and order, we must have more summits, not less, and that the more they talk the better off the world is, and yada yada yada. They scan a world that has increasing wealth creation, relatively full employment, only a handful of localised wars, and now only two of its top fifty countries are not democracies. Life is good. They simply do not understand why there is a sudden widespread and growing alienation.

Let me open my own kimono a bit. I'm a white male of sixty summers. I'm pretty boring. My consistent position through life has been socially liberal and financially conservative. In short, James Dean I am not. But, you know what – I am beginning to share some of the frustrations of the people on the streets.

I have never – ever – felt further away from the politicians elected to represent my interests. I am not alone: barely half the populations of the UK and US actually voted in recent national elections, a terrifying statistic whichever side of the barricade you are on. While our 'elected' politicians pander to the vested interests of those who actually got them there, poverty and functional illiteracy grow daily in the US and the public services crumble in the UK. Add to that the growing influence of global brands, with half the world's top hundred economies now being companies. These entities can now affect populations the size of small and medium-sized countries, but show no signs of democracy. Cut through the rhetoric and they are still driven by earnings per share.

Real power in the world at large is now structured around the Pareto principle – that 80% of power is held by 20% of the players, the latter being a mix of companies and governments. There is no great evil scheme to destroy the world, but these power-brokers are driven by their own agendas. They are the 'haves' – and they want to have more. They pursue cold-eyed logic. Their gods are EVA (economic value added) or market share. Governments are so myopic, sensitive to opinion polls, and openly wired into vested interests that they have become an embarrassment to the common man. None of them is driven by balanced interests, and it has become impossible for the ordinary folk to influence them in any way. That's why the man on the street has become so alienated – in increasing numbers. I despair of this gap being closed. At best, I believe it will get worse before it gets better. Governments may then be forced to remember they are for the people, not just their 'investors'. Brands may also be forced to remember they exist because of their employees and customers, and not just their 'investors'. But don't hold your breath.

You know, I think I do myself an injustice. If the light catches me just right, I look a bit like James Dean might have looked like at sixty. I wonder if I still have my old ski mask?

'12 I SAY, WOULD YOU MIND ... ?'

I love history, particularly its paradoxes.

You can look at history through all colours of lenses. You can be depressed at the lies of omission taught today in the schools of our 'developed' society. You can be outraged at past 'values' that saw shell-shocked seventeen-year-olds summarily executed as 'deserters' during World War One, or 'errant' slaves sawn in half, while still alive, in Atlanta. You can make an objective case that Churchill should have been hanged as a war criminal in 1945. You can also wonder what might have been if some attitudes hadn't changed so fast.

Let me give you the case of Sir Hector MacDonald, commander of the British forces in Ceylon in 1903. He was a Boér War hero, but had been disgraced, exposed as a pederast, and faced a court martial. He was summoned back to England to have a pre-trial meeting with his Field Marshal. From that meeting, he was 'called' to a meeting with King Edward VII. After meeting his monarch, he thoughtfully cut the whole process short by shooting himself. Speculation has it the King suggested this solution – which is ironic, if true, because the King himself had many big appetites, only some of which were to do with food.

I can't help it. I am fascinated by why and how that meeting was staged, and how the hell King Eddie broached the subject. What do you do? Wait until the port (an 1877 Taylor's, I presume) and then lean gently forward, let the first cigar smoke clear, and amiably let it drop:

> '*I say, old bean. Had a chat with the powers that be, and it would be awfully bad sport to let this spot of bother reach the papers. You know, the good name of the Regiment and all that. What ho. Might make sense for all parties if you topped yourself – and sooner rather than later.*'

I can only imagine Mac never blinked or skipped breath:

> '*Absolutely, Your Majesty. Took the words out of my mouth. Great, really great, idea.*'

What has this got to do with modern business? This bizarre incident reflects a time when public figures, faced with failure, were prepared to stand up and accept responsibility, and the ramifications that came with it. The last of these was John Profumo – to my eyes a troubled hero, not an enemy of the State. Not every one of these involved a bottle of whisky and a revolver, and not every one involved scandal. But a public failure was not necessarily seen as dishonourable in an age when honour was still worn as though it was your best suit. No, the dishonour came from the way you handled failure. If you openly accepted responsibility, you didn't try to deflect the blame, and you stepped down from office and disappeared for a while, the chances are that you could rise again. Society at large, and your peers specifically, could forgive an honourable human failing, but they would not forgive a dishonourable attempt to lie, hide, and profit from it.

Now, contrast that with today's business heroes. Over the past few years, a whole gaggle of businesses have failed. It's not the first time a bubble has burst in history – and it won't be the last – but it has been widespread and painful. Investors saw market values tank, pensioners got beached and employees were laid off, again, in thousands. Behind all this were a bunch of business 'leaders', largely in technology businesses, who saw nothing to worry about when their price–earnings ratios were in triple digits, their borrowings (and gearing) were off the graph, their overhead burn-rates were chomping their liquidity and their revenues were a long distant promise.

It is wrong to say their myopic leadership was solely responsible for bringing down this total house of cards, but they were on the bridges of their ships when it happened. Those who suffered when their particular companies crashed had nowhere else to look for responsibility and accountability than at the *grand fromage* who was leading the business at the time. Now then, have there been a bunch of honourable suicides, or – at the very least – some honourable acceptances of guilt and resignations as a result of all these failures and failings? Nah.

Let's take the case of Richard McGinn, who supervised the disintegration of shareholder value in Lucent (along with more than ten thousand jobs) during his three-year time on the ship's bridge. (I could have picked any of fifty – a hundred, maybe – names, from either side of the Atlantic, to make this point.) Resign? I don't think so. The 'price' Mr. McGinn 'charged' for leaving the debacle he had steered Lucent into was (approximately) $13 million, and he is entitled to a long list of future perks, including a near-$1 million annual pension.

There is no public disgrace with these people. They are hidden behind a panel of attorneys. The exit packages are all definitive agreements. Everything is legal.

After a lot of thought, I have concluded that there is no need for these failing people to kill themselves in these sanguine times. But that may need to change soon, and my suggestion to today's business community would be that somebody should take on the role of the King in 1903 – you know, making sensible and sensitive judgements, but being prepared to make an example now and again.

It would work, I know it would – and I am available.

FIRST, FINISH YOUR CHICKEN

I have lived a full and contributive life. It was I who brought all our children back to their senses by inventing, planning, and overseeing the execution of the punk rock movement. I cannot claim full authorship – but it was I, together with a thin, wiry Elvis Costello, back in the seventies, who decided one night, albeit after a jug or two of grappa, that the Moody Blues had become too fat and orchestrated. The rest, of course, is history. Our children were saved.

For many, that would be enough for one lifetime. Not me. Angered by the docility and comfort of the wealth-creating institutions of the eighties, I sat down with another friend, Ivan Boesky, and this time, helped by a decanter of fine port, we planned the whole junk-bond thing. That proved so radical that I had to call in a few IOUs in the White House to stay out of jail. Ivan, of course, was not so lucky.

You would think that reforming the whole youth movement and the basic structures of wealth creation would be enough – but I'm off again. This time I need to sort out these things called 'consumers'. They are becoming their own worst enemies.

I'll start with chicken, move through salmon, and on to airlines. On the way I'll develop a theory. At this stage you'll just have to trust me on that.

The free market is like democracy and the internet. The benefits of all three of them are extensive and obvious, but the pitfalls are significant and usually swept under the rug. All three of them can be defended on the basis that, on balance, we are much better off with them than without them.

One of the tenets of the free market is that competition will provide the required Darwinism. Supply and demand lines will cross on a graph and fix a value for a product or service. If the market is left alone, the aggregate of all those points will optimise the 'welfare' of the maximum possible number of people. The problem is that the common way of measuring value is the price you pay for it, and the increasing assumption is that the cheaper it is, the better it is for the buyer. Therefore, the cheaper it is, the more you will sell of it.

This works well in areas where nobody is actually put at risk or exploited by cheapening the products. But the reality is that the 'hunt for low overhead' increasingly involves exploitative practices (for example, using Third-World labour). In my observation, it can also involve real risks to the ignorant but enthusiastic consumer.

In my childhood, we were neither rich nor poor. A roast chicken, however, was still something of an event in our post-war English house, and tasted delicious. Salmon was a true rarity, costing, as it did, the price of a dozen alternative meals for a pound of it. Air flights were still a dream. Today, all three are virtual commodities. On the surface, that is welcome news for the consumers of the world. It should also be terrifying.

Chicken is cheap. Why? Because, if the average reader knew the true conditions of the battery farming techniques brought into play to make that cheapness possible, they would faint. I am not going to go into detail here – but it is fairly indisputable that at least twenty million battery chickens are killed, world-wide, each day, in a none-too-pleasant way, after about six weeks of a none-too-pleasant life, at the end of which they can just stand up in the space they are allowed after being pumped with growth-promoting antibiotics. Sure, it's cheap. But the only way you can get any flavour in the 'meat' is to coat it with sauce or spices.

Salmon? The 'salmon' on most of our plates today bears no relation to the athletic king of the wild stream that is the true bearer of the name. The natural habitat of most of these 'fish' is a bathful of chemically tainted, louse-and-parasite-infested, excrement-laden, and occasionally toxic seawater. Their diet is mainly colorant. Many of them 'escape' their prison farms and infect their wild cousins. They now threaten the very existence of the real thing. Sure, it's cheap. The cause of that cheapness, however, is such that I will never knowingly eat farmed salmon again.

It's not just food. Air travel is now within the financial reach of most people. What the year 2001 taught us was that a big plane, full of fuel, in the hands of a trained pilot who has a profoundly different opinion on the sanctity of human life than most of us, is a fearful weapon. One of the reasons air flights are so (relatively) cheap, is that the security practices required to completely avoid those circumstances are expensive and, therefore, under-resourced.

Cheapness that involves exploitation and/or risk is not value. In my world, chicken, salmon and air travel (as a *start*) would cease to be commodities. They should be mandated to cost five times as much as they do, and become special again. They would become special again because they could be done properly. We will re-discover what chicken tastes like. We will save up for, and celebrate, a piece of salmon. Air travel will become something you look forward to.

Wow. Is there no stopping me? First, our children, and then wealth creators. Now I've done consumers. Next, I will take on soccer players' salaries, followed by the whole 'bling' concept.

WHAT A LOAD OF HAGGIS

To Scotland – by my calculation, the fiftieth country I have visited. Many of my US readers will not have been there, but most will have mental images of all that wonderful Scottish stuff – kilts, St. Andrews golf course, malt whisky, the Highlands and Mel Gibson. I fell in love with the place twenty-five years ago when my wife and I had a bed-and-breakfast touring holiday in the Western Isles. We were introduced to a concept called 'high tea', and I put on about forty pounds in ten days.

In the winter, it's a bit of an effort for an ex-Florida dweller like me to brave the climate and go there – but I was determined so to do. The event was to celebrate the winners of a bunch of prestigious corporate training awards, and I wanted to hoot and holler my support. In these parlous and difficult times, when discretionary spending budgets have all but disappeared, these companies had been brave enough to raid the corporate coffers to invest in developing their people.

The images of September 11, now almost five years old, are still horribly fresh in our minds, but what happened immediately afterwards seems a bit blurry. There was a load of political rhetoric and military posturing. Consumers changed a lot of buying habits overnight. Financial markets reflected a surge out of equities. Many companies seemed frozen in the headlights, simply – and understandably – not sure of the implications for them. If you re-run your memory-movie, however, you will recall that a few of them moved rapidly and within a couple of days had announced huge layoffs – some of them in double-digit thousands.

Now then, I'm willing to make a bet. If you took those companies that made such a move and scoured their previous corporate communication documents or the transcripts of their shareholder meetings, my bet is you would find the words 'our people are our greatest asset' somewhere in there. So we have this strange pattern of behaviour – if you are suddenly faced with a crisis, you decide to face it *without* your best weapon, i.e. your greatest asset.

Of course, the whole 'greatest asset' thing is a load of haggis (while I'm in Scotland ...). It represents the cynicism of modern business at its worst, and has now overtaken 'empowerment' as the biggest gap between walk and talk in industry today. But I found that particular round of layoffs a wee bit more sinister.

I can tell you, from experience, that mass layoffs are complicated things to do properly. The company's behaviour and actions are, rightly, governed by employee contracts and legal regulation – which varies, sometimes by local statute as well as national law. It needs careful planning, communication and consultation. If a company announces a specific figure of x-thousand layoffs, as a reaction to a specific event, within a couple of days of that event, it tells me that such companies were reading from one of two scripts.

The first script is that the plan already existed in detail, and the company was waiting for an opportune moment, or an appropriate set of circumstances, to put it in the public domain. These would be defined, of course, as circumstances that enabled the company to blame something other than its own woeful performance for the cutbacks. Am I saying some corporate big cheeses actually *welcomed* the September atrocities? Absolutely not. That would be a crass accusation. Am I saying a few took the chance to hide existing bad news behind the chaos? Absolutely.

There is another scenario: a detailed plan didn't pre-exist. In which case the number of announced layoffs had little or no science, thought or planning behind it. The eventual number probably had its genesis in a CEO banging a table and yelling that the company needed ten thousand off the payroll. Now. Today. Two days later, a figure of twelve thousand ('Err on the side of aggression – this may not happen again') is announced – which is no more than a swish in the air in an attempt to address perceived future market slowdown and shareholder paranoia. If you can think of a better way to make the wrong decision for the wrong reason, e-mail it to me.

None of this is new. Most businesses treat employees as the accountants force us to – as expenses, not assets. And I'm not daft enough to suggest that the variable cost of a company's labour force shouldn't be constantly scrutinised to make sure it is effective and efficient. Sometimes you do have to reorganise or restructure your business to reflect rapidly changing circumstances. And, yes, that can involve workforce reductions and it is the right decision for *all* stakeholders. What I'm saying is we need to find a better way to live with that.

In all but a few enlightened and/or small businesses (like the ones I celebrated at the start of this chapter), the employee contract now represents a marriage of convenience. There is little or no loyalty, respect or affection. There is an understanding that one party needs the other to create respective wealth, and a secondary understanding that if either party could do without the other one, it surely would. Personally, I have no problem with that because it reflects the real world. What I would like is way less rhetoric and humbug to suggest something else exists when it palpably doesn't.

Ouch. I have just tried to re-read the last paragraph, and my head hurts. It's the day after my trip to Glasgow. One thing I forgot to mention about the Scots – they know how to party.

PROPHECIES, PROPHECIES

A generation ago, we entered the Age of Aquarius. I remember the moment vividly, as the cast sang about it in a controversial stage musical of the day called *Hair*. It was controversial because the same cast took their clothes off. This nakedness lasted for precisely nine seconds (I timed it), during which time they were bathed in a blue spotlight. This made the men look very cold.

As we entered this exciting new age, many wise people made prophecies. They examined the deep-seated trends of the day and multiplied them by the square root of the *zeitgeist*. It is amazing, as we look back now, just how none of them came to pass. And by how much they missed the mark. Let's have a closer look.

We were all going to enjoy vastly more leisure time. Yup, the plan was that all the technology developments would enable those of us working in the developed and civilised West to cut back on working hours. The primary industries would move over to the developing nations, and we would create the same relative wealth as before by working in money markets or selling pizza for a couple of days a week. *Our big new problem would be knowing what to do with all our new-found leisure time.* People wrote books on this exciting new social challenge. Thirty or forty years later, we are still waiting for it to arrive. If anything, it looks more distant.

What happened, of course, was that the primary industries did disappear, as did large herds of administrative employees. Which left two camps of people – those who kept a job (who found themselves working longer and harder for the same money) and those who lost their jobs (who found themselves doing two or three minimum-wage jobs to survive). And the Age of Aquarius was batting 0 for 1.

Now here's one that was a real banker. It was forecast that women would cease to be women and become *persons*. This would have major social implications in the home, as the career woman would irrevocably change the face of family architecture. It also had huge implications for business. There would be no distinguishing women from men in the workplace, and long-established discriminations would quickly erode and disappear. A quick look at the results indicates 0 for 1 becomes 0 for 2.

Let's take the two fundamental measurements – equal pay and representation at the highest decision-making levels in business. Take pay first: at micro level, on both sides of the Atlantic, each woman's pay level can be justified up the Wahoo. It has to be, legally. But guess what: at the macro level, as a race of Persons, they are still behind. As for boardroom representation, a scan of the top executive positions in the *Fortune* or FTSE list of blue-chip companies shows an alarming stereotype when it comes to key executives: white, male, somewhere around fifty years old, and with a bucketful of stock options. Oh, and while we are at it, the similar prophecies that disabled people and minorities would also make progress, and become persons in this latter category, have also lost a wheel.

Now here's a prophecy that surely must have come good – that we would all become far healthier. The constant whining of do-gooders, the overdose of information on what's good and bad for you, the ready availability of nutritious food all the year round at prices that are afford-able, and the carpet bombing of media with photographs of what you should look like and articles on how you should live was irresistible, *n'est-çe pas?*

Er, no. Highly resistible, actually. Obesity is rising, more kids smoke, diabetes is rampant, the volume of alcohol in-take might be down, but strength is up – and soft drugs are only marginally less common than cheese crackers. During my time on the bridge of the good ship Burger King, we tested putting low-fat mayo on the Whopper. For a week or two, I was on the FBI's most wanted list. So that's 0 for 4.

Aha! But what about telecommuting, I hear you ask. That was forecast, and that surely happened, didn't it? Thousands of administrative workers, previously glued to a chair in a cubicle, now with the freedom to work in their jimjams, would be able to link seamlessly with their Korean suppliers or their German customers while applying oint-ment to little Billy's zits. Er, no, actually. That not only hasn't happened, it shows no sign turning up. Less than one half of one percent of the eligible workforce now telecommute. It would seem that either they don't like it or the company doesn't like it. My theory is that neither of 'em like it. I can understand both points of view: for many workers, there is actually an attraction about leaving the house and having another life with another bunch of people. Sure, they'd like a better balance, with more time at home – but not the Full Monty. As for employers, the benefits of having your people together are perceived to still outweigh the potential real estate savings. 0 for 5.

Poor old Age of Aquarius … but I still love it. One of its attractions is that it has fooled us all. I grew up with an Iron Curtain across Europe that has now gone – quite unbeliev-able, along with many other unpredictable developments. Of course, I don't like all that has happened, from the failure of the forecast breakthrough of women into the boardroom to the nightmare of global terrorism.

On balance, though, it's a wonderful Age, and we should celebrate it. It has certainly taught me some valuable lessons. For example, if circumstances are such that you are inclined to remove your clothes with somebody watching, make sure there is not a blue light on.

DANGER! GENIUS AT WORK

I hit the entrance to big business in the 1970s, armed only with a pair of flared trousers and an MBA. As I remember it, the trousers were of respectable quality and lasted a few months before I discarded them, moving on to the safety pins and rags of punk rock. The MBA, however, lasted only a week or two. It took just that long to realise fancy stuff was of no use in the real world of business. Whenever I mentioned regression analysis, people would blush and turn away as though I had left my flies undone.

As I progressed up the ladder of big business, I found my inspiration in other sources. Strangely, the higher I got, the more the works of the great philosophers played a part. When I reached the shores of the United States, captaining the good ship Burger King, I found that the Stoic school of thinking was suddenly appropriate – summarised here as: *Things will be Bad. Plan on that basis.* Later, my leadership became inspired by the ideas of the gloomy German philosopher, Hegel, summarised here as: *You are born wet, hungry and crying; then it gets worse.*

Over the past few years I have cheered up a bit. Trying to figure out what I wanted to be when I grew up, I read a book by Charles Handy called *The Empty Raincoat.* In it he outlines his thoughts on how the basic structure of business people's lives has changed in the last generation. It used to be three stages – *dependency, job, dependency* – and then the big finish with death. Now, it is more likely to be a four-stage process – dependency, job, *something else*, dependency, and then the Grim Reaper. Many folk are now finding that their basic careers are over – either by their own choice or somebody else's – by the time they are fifty. People are also living longer. There is, therefore, a big gap to fill, which previous generations never had to think about. I'm right slap-bang in it, and loving it.

It's not a big jump to move that thinking on and to align it with another life model theory – again, relatively new. This idea suggests that modern life is like filling a glass with stones. You start with big ones, but you can only get one or two in (main career? main relationship?). When you can't get any more big ones in, you start filling it with smaller ones. Finally, when no more of this size will go in, you finish filling the glass up to the rim with grains of sand.

That's the model I'm following, and I'm at the stage where I'm finding a whole variety of mid-sized stones and jamming them in my glass. It's stuff I'd never contemplated while I was working on the big-stone phase.

Now then, it was only when I'd had my fifth beer (Boddingtons, to be more accurate) that I realised we might have invented a viable business model here. This actually works for the development of many businesses (in general) and brands (in particular).

Let's take my old favourite, Burger King, as an example. The business and the brand were both born in the 1950s, and the founders, Jim McLemore and Dave Edgerton, filled the glass with big stones almost at once. The Whopper flagship sandwich, the chain broiler, and the 'Have it your way' sandwich-making process were in place from the start. Fifty years on, these three still make up the basic building blocks of the system. On the journey, of course, many more stones were added to the glass, although it is arguable that none of them matched the size and significance of those original three. Drive-throughs came along, as did breakfast, chicken products, international development, bundled-up value meals, and kids' marketing – all these, in my mind, making up the mid-sized stones. Dotted around these have been countless marketing initiatives, new product launches, reorganisations, kitchen developments, and so on, which form the grains of sand.

What this theory tells us is that the big, structural elements that give a brand or a business sustainable distinction are usually in place very early, but the journey doesn't stop. There is room to add smaller stuff around the main elements, which enables you to get nearer fulfilling the real potential. And when you are tapped out with those, you can still add the grains of sand – almost ad infinitum.

Just stand back for a minute and look at your own business. Whether it be large or small, it is likely that the 'Big Idea' came at the start and, if you have survived this far, that BI proved distinct and sustainable. Not one BI, however, has stood the test of time without being added to and developed. Even the daddy of 'em all, Coca-Cola, has seen can and fountain technology developments, the introduction of Diet Coke, and a ton of smaller initiatives being added to its glass over the years. Where does your business stand? What's needed? More mid-sized stones? Or are you down to tweaking by adding grains of sand? The bad news is that there is no do-nothing choice. Nobody survives on cruise control today.

I honestly feel that this breakthrough in business modelling may warrant a Nobel Prize of some kind, an honour for which I am long overdue. There is, however, one flaw in my brilliant theory. It relates to my two sons. They actually started their lives filling their glasses with sand, they have stayed with sand, and, it would seem, intend to stay with sand. Their message to me, written in sand, is this: *Sand is cool. So shove your theory where the sun don't shine.*

THE WEEK THAT WAS

We writers stand accused of two crimes against humanity. First: when we are excited by an idea, we often witter on for ages in pursuit of a full stop. Second: we whine a lot. I'm currently in the latter mode.

Here's the problem. You will be reading this quite some time after I've written it. This normally precludes me writing about anything too date-specific. Frankly, there's nothing worse than reading stuff that can only see its shelf life in the rear-view mirror. Two things happened during a recent week, however, that are giving me an excuse to break the rule. So please bear with me.

The week was the second week in February, 2002, when we saw Kenneth Lay, late of Enron, holding up his hand in front of members of the elected government of the United States and hiding behind his mum's apron – whoops, I mean pleading the Fifth Amendment. In the same week, Anita Roddick lost control of her business. She was founder and, until then, the principal conductor of one of the world's best-known brands: The Body Shop (which has now been sold).

We witnessed the simultaneous fall of two business leaders. What made it doubly interesting was that they represented two entirely different styles of leadership.

You don't want to get me started on Lay and his hench-
men, but let's just say they represent the Adam Smith–Gordon Gekko-Darwinistic–free market–everybody wins if
everybody pursues their own vested self-interest–exploitative–greedy–share-price driven version of capitalist leadership.

Anita rowed a different boat. Profit, personal greed and
(unfortunately) investor returns were all low priorities. She
saw 'her' business as a vehicle that would drive the world to
a better place. The cynics would have it that The Body Shop
was simply an exercise *in extremis* of cause-related marketing – but her consistent track record shows she sought to use
'her' business to lighten Third-World oppression and ease
the battering the environment is taking from our presence.
In addition, she used her own high business profile to support worthy non-business causes. She epitomised the model
that recognises that a business needs to reflect the interests
of many stakeholders.

Both of these figures fell from grace in the same week,
which raises the question: just where do we point our children when they ask for business leadership role models?

The definition of the point when you've become old, for
a male, is when you first save a piece of wood to stir paint
with in the future. I have been doing that a lot recently. Now,
has age brought me wisdom, particularly in this contentious
area? It certainly has.

My views on this subject are now geometrically in line
with those of Mort Meyerson. Mort was, you will remember, a kind-of joint commander of the business giant EDS,
together with that strange little ET-like creature who nearly became president of the US. Together they espoused a
sternly Protestant style of leadership, but that is not what
has inspired this reference. I am much more impressed with
Mort's magazine article from a couple of years back. Its

contents are summarised in its title: *Everything I Thought I Knew About Leadership Is Wrong*. Bingo.

In truth, that's where most of us are. The whole leadership thing has got so complex, and brings so much pressure, that about 95% of all our preconceived ideas are capable of being proved wrong. Leaders we admire as lions crash and burn in just the same way as those we think of as donkeys. All bets are off.

You will note I said '95%'. Floating about in the 5%, where we can retain some confidence, are a couple of leadership must-haves that not only still survive but seem to me to be increasing in importance. They are not new and they are not fancy, but my advice is not to leave your leadership home without them.

The first is personal integrity. I cannot see any leadership model today, if built on deceit, surviving over anything but the short term. Whether it is an exercise in 'supporting' your share price, or simply dealing with your employees, customers or affected outside parties, you will get found out today if you try to deceive. You will not necessarily be tumbled by regulation, auditors, or GAAP. These bodies are all capable of missing this stuff. But there is simply too much information available that cannot be hidden all the time from all the people who sing from a different hymn sheet. With the World Wide Web in place, there is nowhere to hide.

The second is to learn from the Orient. In the East, a good deal is where both parties leave the table smiling. A four or five on the dice is okay; it doesn't have to be six every time. So, deal something back. Re-invest in a partnership. Surprise a customer by giving something away proactively and/or without pressure. Don't rape suppliers just because you can. Treat your employees as assets, not expenses. When you look outside your tent, show the world you give a damn.

None of this means you turn into Mother Teresa. To be an effective modern leader, you cannot build just on the cornerstones of popularity and being a nice guy. And Anita Roddick's fade-out reminds us that the prime purpose of being in business remains the capture and retention of a customer, not a supplier. But you can succeed without deceit and without having to take the whole pot at every visit to the table.

I know, I know – such wisdom from one so young. But the world is full of new 'wisdoms'. Another one that spoils breakfast for some folk is the maxim that you are not actually a millionaire until *you have sold the stock and paid the taxes*.

18

GO ON, SURPRISE ME:
MAKE MY DAY

Despite the fact that the last twenty-five years have seen an alarming increase in the number of things about which I know nothing, I try and steer a course in life that avoids surprises. I follow Leibowitz's law, for example, which states that when hammering a nail you will never hit a finger if you hold the hammer with both hands.

Life does, of course, insist in throwing occasional spanners in the works. Only yesterday, to give you another working example, I opened a tin that clearly said 'evaporated milk' on the label only to find it was still there. In general, however, I avoid the stresses caused by events not following a predetermined script.

It was only recently that I realised that this approach might be the cause of me missing out – and that a life-plan that drifted towards the other end of the spectrum might also provide an effective and efficient business tool.

The setting for this epiphany was a restaurant in Florida. Two of us were eating and were some way through a meal that was – as planned – unsurprising. The place was thinly populated, but there was nothing in the food, ambience, decor or service that had so far generated any sort of comment – either of praise or criticism. All that was about to change. We were positioned near the kitchen door, which slowly opened. A guy in a dark suit walked through into the restaurant area. Without any drama, he approached our table and asked us how the meal had been. In fairness, we both had to think, as the whole experience had been singularly unmemorable, but when it all came back to us it seemed to be OK, so we passed on the good news. His brow furrowed. Barely controlling his emotions, he startled us with a short, but memorable, speech: 'It may have seemed OK, but let me assure you, I am not happy with anything in this place tonight. It does not come up to my standards. The meal is on the house.' With that he turned on his heels and headed off towards the next occupied table – leaving us open-mouthed, and not a little worried about what we had just eaten.

After a lot of post-match analysis, and having survived the night with no negative side-effects, we decided that we were a lot more impressed than concerned. It seems we had dined at a restaurant run by the last person on earth who was both honest and uncompromising – and who was prepared to lose unnecessary money in the pursuit of both values. What a surprise – a pleasant one.

It's this 'pleasant surprise' thing that got me thinking. Most of us would confess to a natural dislike of being surprised, but what we mean, of course, is that we dislike being *unpleasantly* surprised. That attitude arises because that's all we ever get. The world is now geared to bland uniformity via the spread of global brands. Add to that the fact that the whole business universe is involved in a master plan to lower our expectations so that we are not unpleasantly surprised every two minutes. If you book a flight, for example, you might see a take-off scheduled at 10.15 a.m. and an arrival at 12.15 p.m. – that's a flight time of two hours. When you eventually take off, however, the pilot tells you that the flight time will be one hour and fifteen minutes. So, what's with the 'missing' forty-five minutes? It's easily found: their whole act is so *crappola* that they need this to cover for routine inefficiencies. In this way, if you plan around their published times, you get no unpleasant surprises. If they do have a tail wind and arrive at the gate at 11.40 p.m. – i.e. 'early' – you think you've won a minor prize in the Lottery.

It's not just airlines: they are *all* doing it, trust me. Try ringing up the phone company and navigating your way through the hold-menu. Try calling a plumber. Have you ever tried to correspond with a big private or public sector organisation? The whole process is shaped to lower your expectations to a level where you get no unpleasant surprises. Occasionally, if they do something half-right, you are anaesthetised to such a degree that you believe you have beaten the system and are pleasantly surprised.

Let's go back to our troubled restaurateur, and see if he's unknowingly come up with a business weapon we could all use – one that is also efficient, effective and cheap. I think he has. The key is that what he did was not just a pleasant surprise, but that it was also proactive. No only did he surprise us pleasantly – part of the effectiveness was that it came before we were expecting anything – but it also came from right out of the blue and was mighty powerful. So, let's call it the PPS – the pleasant proactive surprise.

It doesn't have to be expensive, and it doesn't have to be related to something going wrong. One of the most successful franchisees we had in my time with Burger King was Manny Garcia in south Florida. Sure, he had good locations and a reasonably wealthy market – but so did many others. I'm not daft enough to put his overall success just down to a couple of tiny PPSs, but his staff used to go round the restaurants with free coffee fill-ups and mints, and there was enough positive feedback from that alone that convinced me it contributed. Here's the power of what I am talking about – the PPS is so rare in modern business life, it's actually exhilarating when you get one. What's important is that you do tend to go back to a business that gives you such an experience.

It's a powerful weapon because *nothing surprises us any more*. If I told you there are twice as many plastic flamingos in south Florida as real ones, you wouldn't be at all surprised would you? Amazingly, you would be right not to be.

THE DEFENCE SPEAKS

I belong to an elite club. Membership consists of ex-Burger King CEOs. At the last count there were only 175,397 of us still alive.

As Club VP for External Relations, I have a responsibility. The fast-food industry has come under heavy mortar fire from a journalist by the name of Eric Schlosser in his book *Fast Food Nation*. We need a response.

In no particular order of priority, the industry stands accused of fuelling mass obesity, losing a better way of life, exploiting labour and consumers (particularly children in both camps), abusing power, being pathetically regulated, advancing new diseases, unfairly distributing wealth, and over-globalising the planet. After reading it I felt like Pol Pot.

What an absolute crock.

I cannot attempt a detailed debate in a few paragraphs. That's even if I wanted to – and I don't. The truth is that there is much about the industry that should give everybody in it cause for concern, and objective challenge should be welcomed. But a full debate needs two added dimensions that the book doesn't provide.

First, it needs balance. In and of itself, the book is a powerful piece of scholarship – but in my observation a piece of work is better if the conclusions come after the research. In this case there is the strong feeling that the author's mind was set and the extensive research was an exercise in finding and selecting stuff to support that position. Any industry that provides work and affordable food for many millions of people every day; that creates wealth; that is consistent and relatively safe and that is regulated in the main by elected governments cannot be all bad. That's all missing, and what the book also fails to do is to define the alternatives. Presumably they are omitted because they only exist someplace over the rainbow.

The second issue I have with Schlosser's thesis is that it addresses the symptoms, not the disease. The problem with this planet is that its population has forward momentum. People keep inventing things. People want more for themselves. The strong exploit the weak because they can. These forces drive societal and economic changes, which bring a lot of benefits – and a lot of costs. Sure, it would be nice to pick and choose – but you can't. The momentum is always forward. The benefits always come, but then we are all faced with managing the costs whether we like it or not.

Schlosser is right. There are some aspects of the fast-food industry that are hideous and that cannot be defended. But they are not specifically about fast food. They are about the cost of the planet's development momentum and the imperfections of its population. Here are some examples:

- *Abuse of juveniles as employees* – There are regulations with which society feels comfortable, and there will be more. The real abuse comes from those little Hitlers who use their local power to run their operations like something out of a Dickens novel. They abuse regulations and people because they can get away with it, and they exist in every industry.

- *Abuse of children as consumers* – When I was a kid, you could have marketed to me until the cows came home. If my parents didn't think it was right for me, it was off limits. The crass abdication of parental responsibility is a society-wide disease. Burger King Kids Club is not the real problem here, trust me.
- *Obesity* – In Europe and the USA alone, more than 500 million people need two to three meals a day. The fast-food industry makes millions of meals available at affordable prices. If they didn't, I don't know who else would. Now then, it is no big secret that some foods you eat during a week have different dietary properties. Some folk eat too much, have too many meals, and have the wrong mix in their diet. Is this really a supply-side problem? No. So, eat less and/or eat better. It is an entirely discretionary consumer decision.
- *Low wages* – Whether the minimum wage is where it is now, or twenty times higher, or doesn't exist at all, there will always be a bunch of jobs in society that are (by definition) at the bottom of the pay league. They are defined by where consumer supply and demand, and labour market supply and demand, all come together at one point on society's welfare graph. And, yes, fast food is there with a group of others. But guess what – it is not entirely a bad thing. It provides a wealth of opportunities for the low-skilled and itinerant. It provides an entry point for those who can and want to develop. It has helped millions of students make ends meet on a journey that otherwise might have been impossible. And for those (like me) who are lucky enough to progress in life, it provides a workplace experience that should make you a more empathetic and sensitive manager of those less fortunate.

Schlosser had 288 pages. I've got loads more ammo, but I'll stop after a couple. Fast food ain't the real problem. Schlosser's the real problem – inasmuch as he exists on the planet with six billion peers. Their aspirations and needs create demand forces that are supplied by people. As such they are occasionally subject to greed and abuse, and are occasionally out of control.

If we could cure those diseases, it would be an historic first. Meanwhile, it's a wonderful world with a lot of faults. We could and should try to do better.

I haven't had one for a year, but I suddenly feel like a Whopper.

AND NOW FOR SOMETHING
COMPLETELY DIFFERENT

With a start I realise it is over a decade since I left my position as the Anna Kournikova of Big Business. From the minimal research I have done on the subject, it seems nobody missed me. Few people, apart from my bank manager, evidenced any distress at the time. Had he actually been dead, he assured me, he would have accorded me the honour of turning in his grave.

I have never missed that world for a minute. Others who have left it have felt the need to justify the move – 'wanting to spend more time with the family' being a favoured reason. I simply decided that after a quarter of a century of bosses, I would never work for anybody again.

I have survived, without the covering fire of a big corporation and a pay cheque, thanks to the rigid application of a three-part formula I designed at the time. The three elements are deceptively simple: 1) make a lot of lists; 2) forget one person every day; and 3) track nothing but cash flow. It was only with the wisdom afforded me by ten years of hindsight that I realised that if I had applied these rules while I was a big cheese, I would have been a far better CEO. Let me expand.

It was Tom Peters, I think, who said, '*If you've got more than one priority, you got none.*' Forgetting the massacre of the English language, this always struck me as sound advice. I followed it, as I know thousands of other managers did – and still do. Today, however, I start every day with a new Post-It note, listing at least twenty tiddly things with which I must occupy my time. Some days I have two lists. Some days I have lists of lists. I suddenly realised this is actually a magnificent way to run a business – because having the Single Great Big Priority From Hell is now far too inflexible for modern needs.

Business is so multidimensional and fast-changing, my new way is the only way to map your journey. Besides, if you have no real idea about your priorities, *your competitors won't have a clue*. This is now the only way to stay ahead of the market. Also, if you can change priorities on a dime, and actually forget or lose some, you can avoid the *SMEF* (spontaneous massive existence failure) that is so popular among many of today's global giants.

The next element is a lot more subtle – forget one person every day. I invented this because of worries about my memory. I have an outstanding ability to remember the names of all the Kinks, but an outstanding inability to remember somebody I met yesterday. Clearly, I am heading for short-term memory troubles in my later years, so this tactic was devised to get there first. In this way, I will be in control. So I work hard and deliberately sit down and forget somebody every day.

Eureka! I found I had stumbled on another winning management strategy. We all know far too many people and constantly try to remember more. We (particularly males) need to stop trying to impress. We need to figure out who is important to us and to whom we mean something special. The reality in modern business is that there are about fifteen people who are personally mission-critical to most of us. These are the relationships that need working on and nurturing. One by one, you should forget the rest. You will see things much more clearly, and you will be sure-footed and pleasant to be with.

Thirdly, ignore everything else – just track the cash. I was given advice once by a veteran in the brewing industry when I was head-hunted for a job he thought he should have landed. Effectively, I ended his career by being brought in over his head, but he still had the class to try and help me. He told me that if anybody wanted to learn about a business quickly they should sign every cheque and read every pay-ing-in slip for a couple of weeks.

I ignored it then but recognise it now as a jewel of advice. I run my life on a cash-accounting basis – and if I ever re-joined big business, I would monitor little else. One of the fundamental cancers in business is now the ability to lie, through and over (and, in some cases, abetted by) auditors and present GAAP accounts that actually show what the profits would have been if the company hadn't paid its bills, created a 'restructuring charge' or invested in e-commerce. The only solution is for the world to move to cash accounting for its primary presentation of results, with all the other *crappola* attached as appendices. Forget paper valuations and non-cash items. Forget the difference between balance sheets and operating statements. If you've spent it, it's gone. If you've received it, you can use it. Nothing else matters.

There is a possibility that I have completely revolution-ised the combined science and art of business management with these discoveries. There may be a book – and possibly a film – in it for me. All I can say is that these ideas work for me, and I wish I'd thought of them twenty-five years ago. You might want to give 'em a go.

Now then, I can see there are the sceptics among you who believe I am pulling everybody's leg – that this excit-ing new approach is just a joke to fill a chapter. The only way I will dignify such comments with a response is to echo

Peter Cook's wonderful words to Dudley Moore in the film *Bedazzled*: 'Everything I have told you so far is a complete lie. *Including that.*'

MEDIOCRE, SAD
AND CHEATING:
THE ASCENT OF MAN

For many years now my wife has been immersed in the wondrous world of genealogy. For almost as many years I left her and it well alone, thinking, mistakenly, that it was all about the mysteries of female reproductive organs. Apparently, that is a science that sounds similar, and this one is actually about family trees. Phew.

Once I knew that, there was no stopping me. Within days I had traced the living descendants of Alexander the Great (356–323 BC), Frederick the Great (1712–1786) and Alfred the Great (871–900). Out of respect for their privacy, I won't tell you their addresses or phone numbers – but let me tell you who they are and what they are doing.

The 71st generational descendant of Alexander the Great has the same given name, but his full name is now Alexander the Mediocre. He works in my bank's call centre.

I have been with the bank for about thirty-five years, and I have reached the stage in life where I qualify for the esteemed title of *high net worth individual*. If I want to telephone my bank, however, I have to ring in to a call centre – which I suspect is somewhere in northern India. Before any conversation happens, I then have to tell this latter-day Alex my mother's maiden name, which is a security code I've apparently agreed to. The trouble is I have had a mother and a stepmother and can't remember which one's name I gave. The minute I hesitate, I am treated as though they have heard a leper's bells over the phone. Here's what I should do to Alex – I should tell him to stuff his bank. However, I can't be bothered. It will be a pain to relocate my accounts – and all the other banks will be the same anyway. I suspect that this pathetic attitude (of mine) is the glue that keeps 90% of modern customer relationships alive.

The seventh linear descendant of Frederick the Great is also called Fred. In his case it is Fred the Saddo, and he has many siblings and cousins. You realise what this is about when you ask him about his job.

For thousands of years, people have used a summary narrative of the products and/or services of their labours to describe their jobs (farmer, carpenter, train driver, pizza salesman, etc., etc.). On the surface, Fred the S and his siblings all do such work, but in reality their 24/7 job is to do nothing but manipulate their company's share price. It doesn't matter a fig to them what products and services they market – all that matters is the share price of their company. Their life is a constant flow of spin-doctorship, press releases, PR and misinformation. Now, there's nothing new in propping up a share price, of course, but the past twenty years have seen stock become a key weapon in mega-acquisitions and executive pay. That has changed everything. The result is that thousands – millions – of employees focus on nothing other than stuff that will directly or indirectly keep the company stock in some anti-gravitational hover-mode. What a miserable, sad way to earn a living.

Now, Alfred the Great's modern direct descendant is of an entirely different kidney. You can spot it in his name, which is Alfred the Cheat. I will tell you exactly where he works – in the finance department of my mobile phone service supplier. These phones are a bit like wire coat-hangers in that if you leave two of them in a cupboard overnight, they breed. So we now have several of the things, all with this company.

Like many lazy guys, I pay my mobile phone bill by standing order and just track the total cost as it passes across my breakfast table each month. On one 'slow news' day, however, I read it out of curiosity and discovered that I was paying about £2.50 per month, per machine, for something called 'handset insurance'. There are two points to note here: First, the handsets cost nothing and would cost nothing to replace in a market where suppliers are getting desperate. Second, when I checked, it was quite clear, in all three contracts, that the provision of handset insurance (or any other optional extras) was excluded from the signed contract.

What we have here is sinister. Big Al is sitting in his office, unilaterally adding out-of-contract extras to customer bills – in the hope they won't be noticed. Now, if I contracted to sell someone some timber, and then unilaterally added the price of insurance for it when the contract specifically omitted doing so, and then I took the money anyway, wouldn't I be a cheat? What say you, Al?

When they are caught out, as in my case (and you might want to check yours, right here, right now), they agree to stop it immediately. If you are the one consumer in a thousand who could be bothered to force the issue, I suspect they might reimburse you a few pounds. And why wouldn't they? I suspect this game-plan is netting them millions – and a few payoffs to keep it quiet would be money well spent.

So, there they are – the direct descendants of three of history's great men. One is mediocre, one is sad, and one is a cheat.

It was Jacob Bronowski who summarised the last few thousand years as the Ascent of Man. Not in the case of these three it wasn't.

WHEN I'M SIXTY-FOUR

I am now, of course, of a particular vintage and thus able to see things differently. When I say 'vintage' I do not have in mind the word 'old'. I have in mind a shining Aston Martin of indeterminate years, kept in spectacular condition, or a bottle of 1963 Taylor's Port.

Having been born in the first month of the first full year of peace after the Second World War, I am finding that, with the passage of time, my views are changing on many things. I am, for example, now set firm in my hatred of all things to do with Christmas. I am deeply critical of almost all elected leaders in business, politics and religion – strongly adhering to Steinbeck's view that all nations are to be admired while all governments are to be despised. I detest all this emotional incontinence that now sweeps vast tracts of the developed world when faced with the ugly reality of the latest manifestation of man's inhumanity to man. I frequently accuse modern populist media of insanity. I deplore the basic inequalities of opportunity still institutionalised in everyday life. And I am revolted by the mere thought of French beans.

All these views of mine are secure, objective and well-received at dinner parties, but one area still leaves me confused. This aging process – which has clearly left me an intellectual pygmy and an emotional bigot – must have implications for business leadership. I can't, however, for the life of me figure them out.

When I started in business, the role model for leadership was easy to define. It was a white male aged fifty-plus – or a WMAFP. In America it was all the above, but with the addition of white sprayed hair (i.e. a WMAFPWWSH). This applied if you ran a small business (e.g. a single restaurant) or a massive one (e.g., an international chain of them).

This seemed to run against the conventional wisdom evident in many other occupations – even those that did not depend on young athleticism or beauty as their core competence. Niels Bohr argued that no physicist had ever produced any significant original thinking after the age of 25, and there are many scientists who share a similar view where it concerns their chosen field. Quite obviously, with the possible exception of Bruce Springsteen, nobody has written a modern song of any substance after they were 30. In Mozart's case he did little of merit after becoming a teenager. Despite all this evidence pointing to another option, however, the WMAFPs and the WMAFPWWSHs continued to rule unchallenged in the world of business.

Challenges – or, rather, challengers – appeared at last in the 1990s. The male factor was challenged by the emergence of a new breed of female leaders and entrepreneurs, and the white factor by a similar group of non-whites. The fifty-plus thing then came under heavy fire from a new group of business movers and shakers, who seemed barely out of high school.

The new generation was epitomised by Ernst Malmsten and Kajsa Leander, the six- and eight-and-a-half-year-old Scandinavian 'leaders' of the infamous BOO.com – the deceased and unmourned internet company. Not only did these two signal the death of the old ways, they rubbed salt in the wounds by getting herds of previously sanguine

WMAFPWWSHs to invest millions and millions in their doomed company. It seemed the Age of Aquarius was over at last.

Not so. The oldies fought back. Most of those dotcom enterprises imploded, and the WMAFPs are back in position. Scan any Western corridor of power, and non-whites and women are still noticeable by their absence, and the keys to the top-floor toilets are back in the hands of those with 'experience'. Quite so.

Is there anything in this cycle for quick-service to learn? Is it better to have a white-haired business leader, who has seen it all before and who trades off some fire and creativity for safety and calmness under fire? Or is it a young person's game, with success dependent on the ability to work eighty-hour weeks and be 'in touch' with the market?

My observation is aimed at being oh-so-helpful. It is neither and both. Sure, it is helpful to be physically fit – but there are many people who are in their sixties who are fitter than the sedentary teenagers of today. Sure, intelligence (as against intellect) helps – but I've seen that present in many twenty-year-olds and missing in industry veterans.

The quick-service business is unique in both its range of offerings and its range of people who can succeed at all levels. It does require one particular consistency, and that has nothing to do with age. It requires a mind that has a unique – almost telepathic – insight into the mind of the customer. Because of its very nature, quick-service lives on compromise – and the winning leader knows what is wanted, what is acceptable, and what is off-limits. The trite, conventional rulebook is baloney. The customer, for example, is not always right. To take one case, it is inexcusable for families with young children to leave the restaurant table and floor looking like a hurricane has passed through. The brats (and by that I mean the adults) should be taken out and soundly beaten by a *sous* chef.

The customer, however, always wants one thing – to be treated as you, the owner/manager/leader, would want to be treated if you were in their shoes. If you understand that, and deliver on that, you will succeed – irrespective of age, gender, race, or hair colour.

I have one more piece of advice for WMAFPs, if you are to hold on to power. It is an inviolate law. The arrival of nose hair should signal the disappearance of all visible jewellery. It is mission-critical if you are to remain credible.

TRATTORIAS, OSTERIAS AND BIG QUICK-SERVES

Over the years I have refused offers to eat sea slug and to drink the (still warm) blood of a krait (a staggeringly poisonous snake). These were not offered to me on the same night or, indeed, in the same country, but in both cases they were accompanied by a hint that the off-putting appearance of the delicacies was compensated for by their unquestioned aphrodisiac benefits. My wife gave me full marks for both decisions.

As I reflected on such events, however, it occurred to me that I should make this chapter more international. There is a tendency to think of the quick-serve business as essentially American and where it does appear in the rest of the world, it is where McDonald's or one of the USA's usual-suspect brands makes an appearance. Indeed, if you ask Londoners what a QSR is, they will probably reply that they don't know – but that they think they lost 2–1 on Saturday. The confusion here, of course, is that there is an English soccer team called QPR, which coincidentally means nothing outside England (and actually very little in it). If you are all clear on that, I'll proceed.

My logic in deciding to put an occasional international dimension to this *magnum opus* is that, wherever I have been in the world, cheap and quickly available local food has been readily in evidence – and, indeed, is usually part of the way of life. In many cases, of course, it now co-exists alongside the big US brands, but it is alive and well and there are many lessons that both groups could learn from the other.

Let me start in Tuscany, and more specifically in Florence. It was here the world came out of the Dark Ages via the Renaissance, and some elements of Tuscan culture have gone on to affect the world at large. If you are paid a salary, the genesis of that was when Tuscans were paid in salt (*sale*). This commodity was so precious that taxes were paid on its use, which is why Tuscans dry their tomatoes in the sun and dry their *braesola* beef in the air. It is also why, to this day, they (uniquely, in my experience) use no salt in baking their bread – which is why it tastes like your underpants.

From the top of the hill to the southwest of the city, you can look back down and savour the magnificent panorama. If you do that, the chances are that you will notice something that should be pinned up in every quick-serve boardroom in the world: *there are no visible brand signs*. With tourists topping up a hefty city population, there is a lot of quick-serve food being eaten. With the local pasta and pizza shops, tiny *trattorias* and *osterias*, and the big QSR brand guys all operating inside the city limits, there are a lot of quick-serves. But if you half-close your eyes and look at this glorious city, it seems to have paid no visual price. There are no ugly brand signs. Somehow, it all seems to work without having been turned into a cultural Chernobyl. Now, here's an exam question: compare and contrast that picture with an average American Strip Center or a UK shopping mall. Quite.

Tuscan food raises a couple of other questions that the conventional quick-serve industry could ponder. If quick-serve is what it says – a quick-service concept (as against quick-preparation or quick-eating) – then arguably this part of the world has spawned a worldwide quick-serve industry with thousands and thousands of unbranded pizza/pasta parlours and *trattorias* all over the planet. What they have managed to do in many of these, however, is something that most quick-serve brands gave up decades ago – which is to defend culture, heritage, and integrity.

There is an east–west line drawn across Europe, south of which whole life patterns are determined by the harvest cycles of the olive tree and the grape vine. Obviously, what used to be rural ways of life have extensively changed in industrialised and modernised societies, and the farming techniques themselves bear no relation to those of the past. But a culture remains, and there is a reverence and respect for food and drink, the quality of the ingredients and the *process* involved in eating and drinking. That has been lost elsewhere. I defend the conventional quick-serve industry as vigorously as anyone for the good job it does. But it is about eating to live. Somehow, south of Europe's Olive Line, however cheap and quick the offering, people still live to eat.

You will have gathered that I love Tuscany. It is a delightful and continual paradox. An eternal Italian talent is to make the impossible seem easy, and the easy seem impossible. The stunning buildings – many upwards of a thousand years old – leave you with your jaw firmly dropped. Then you go back to the hotel, and the water in the shower refuses to acknowledge gravity.

Prego.

WHAT I KNOW;
WHAT I DON'T KNOW

The quick-service business is, at times, murderously frustrating to write about. It is full of paradox. It is a bit like the Italy I talked about in the previous chapter – making a few complex things look easy but a lot of easy things far too complex. After a quarter of a century in and around the industry, I have decided that the more I know about it, the less I understand. To bring some order to my intellectual chaos, I decided to run an inventory check on my observations.

I was led to do so by the memory of Mayor Giuliani's speech on 9/11. Frankly, I hadn't been inspired by the guy before and (even more frankly) have not been over-inspired by him (or his truly awful book) since, but cometh the hour, cometh the man. For a while there, he was great leadership personified. In particular, his 'This is what I know, this is what I don't know' speech rang out like a bell amidst the chaos of that dreadful day.

So, after twenty-five years, this is what I know, and what I don't know, about quick-service:

- I do know that if you want to be mass-market in the quick-service business, and that if you seek your market distinction on the back of being healthy and/or fresh, you will fail.

- The minute you go into any foodservice establishment, everybody makes a simple judgement about it way before anything is served. *I have seen research that says this is done in the first two seconds.* More often than not, it is done subconsciously – you are either positive about the place or negative. Once you have formed such an opinion, it takes some changing. I do not know the formula to describe how individuals make that judgement, or even the variables involved. If I did, I would be scary-rich.

- I do know that you should, as a rule, back your employees up. I do know that the customer is not always right.

- I do know that if you see a huge sign outside a quick-service location offering a price-pointed product promotion, when you get inside you will have difficulty finding it. I do know that because I may have been part of the team that invented it. It's called bait and switch in another guise.

- I do know that you can pay £80 per head for a meal and feel you have received great value. I also know that you can pay £2.50 and feel you have been ripped off.

- I do know that the explosion of quick-service branded materials and products inside schools is wrong. And, yes, Burger King pioneered it on my watch – *mea culpa.* And it's happening in Europe as well as the US.

- If Jim McLemore and Ray Kroc were starting Burger King and McDonald's today I do not know that they would seek to grow by franchising. What was an obvious and eminently effective way of rapidly growing a capital-intensive brand half a century ago may not be the right way to do it today. While still using OPM (other people's money), Starbucks has shown that external investors in a company-run system can be a more-than-viable alternative to the franchisee-operator model.

- I met Jim McLemore several times and I do know that, amidst a million faces that have come and gone in my time in business, none has been more friendly or gracious.

- More than fifteen years ago, working for GrandMet, we acquired a pasta-based restaurant brand in Switzerland. Apart from the manager, the restaurant staff were paid either Swiss minimum wages, or a pool of money equivalent to 25% (I think) of the monthly net sales to share – whichever was the highest. The staff were, therefore, understandably motivated to optimise customer spending, to get them to come back again, and to keep staff numbers down. There was a waiting list for jobs at the place. I do not know why this (or something like it) hasn't caught on – everywhere.

- I do know that Starbucks could improve same-store sales by fixing its food act.

- I do know that quick-service exists in some form or other in every country I have visited. I also know that the US is unique – in that every other country somehow emphasises ingredients. You might still be able to recognise them, or maybe the original colours and flavours come through. Maybe the product shape retains some original ingredient identity. Maybe they just tell you (proudly) about the quality of them. One way or another, they manage it.

- I do know that quick-service success is cyclical. Throughout their history, the big brands have responded to new initiatives, pushed forward for a few years and then found that they needed another 'goosing'. Drive-throughs, breakfasts, value-menus, kids' deals, *big* new products – all these have done the job at milestone points in each brand's history. I also know that the cycles are getting shorter, that there's another impetus overdue and that what it is ain't obvious.

Quick-service has its vehement critics. Fair enough – millions have died defending the right to free speech, so you can just rant away, guys. But, can you also tell us what the alternative is? Just how will – literally – billions of people, using quick-service in one form or another, get fed every day? If there is an alternative, this is what I *really* don't know.

LISTEN 'TIL I TELL YOU

Browsing through statistics recently, as I do frequently on your behalf, I came across a stunner. There are, apparently, 275 million people resident in the US, and only fifteen of them have passports. Of that fifteen, only six have actually been abroad, three of those reluctantly to a family wedding in Denmark. I see it, therefore, as a key role of this chapter to expand the international outlook of the stay-at-homes. Today we hit Ireland.

My father was born in Limerick, while I was born in England. The latter fact enables me to see right through the drivel that manifests itself through a million Irish myths that have spread themselves none too thinly across the planet. The former means it is a land, and they are a people, that can grab and inspire me.

From its first examination, Ireland provides a powerful business model for quick-serves. My wife was born in Wales, and I have got to know that country well, along with the land of my father. Now, consider this: Wales and Ireland are about the same size, both have fine hills, verdant valleys, lovely rivers and golden beaches, and both have a powerful cultural heritage, particularly in music and literature. However, whereas Ireland is known (and is usually present in some form) right across the planet, Wales remains one of its best-kept secrets.

A similar law applies to restaurants. You find that if you compare two that *seem* to be the same in most things, they emerge as having very different profiles for no obvious reason. Well, it's not an accident. Here's how Ireland does it in the national comparison with Wales. There are two elements to the game plan, the first being to seek *the sympathy vote*. If you want this route to success in the foodservice business, just plead victimisation and/or suppression endlessly and repetitively. Potato famine, poverty, the English – they are the ones that work for Ireland, but you will, of course, have to find your own for your own market.

The second skill is a bit trickier to master. You have to be able to *make up songs about your misery while you are singing them*. And you do this at 10.00 p.m. every night, wherever you are. It never fails.

It takes time, but if you can master both these elements, you can cut your conventional marketing budget by half.

Zooming in, we will concentrate on wonderful, wonderful Dublin, ignoring the faux Disneylands like Killarney. We will find there are lessons for quick-serves everywhere. First, we find that America does not sell bacon – that hardy annual of many QSR dishes. Oh, America sells something *called* bacon, but if you pop in a Bewleys (est. 1894) and have a full breakfast, you will find two things – first, that your centre of gravity has dropped about eighteen inches after it and, second, bacon in the rest of the world (generally) and Ireland (specifically) has different DNA from the cremated Post-It notes that are served under its name in the US. Bacon rashers are actually big and thick and tasty.

Now then, walk up O'Connell Street and go right past that damned Post Office still scarred with the bullet holes of the 1916 Easter Rising. (All that proves is that no one nation has a monopoly on idiocy.) Keep going north, walking about another twenty minutes. You will come to a quiet square of tall, terraced buildings, one of which houses the Literary Museum. Pay your money and lose yourself in there for a couple of hours. Everywhere around you there are marriages – marriages of unbridled minds and a wondrous command of the language. Read Yeats' poem (at least three times) about 1916. Whatever your politics or religion, if the hairs on the back of your neck do not stand on end, you are dead. Then lighten up by reading an anthology of Miles na Gopaleen's mid-century columns in the *Irish Times*, and cry laughing.

What's this to do with quick-service? Well, when you emerge from the Museum, blinking in the light, you will have changed. You will have morphed into a temporary un-paid Irishman (no matter your gender). Without radar, your feet will lead you straight to Ryan's Bar, and further into one of the 'snugs' at the back. Here you will have a genuine Dublin quick-service meal – seven pints of Guinness, each about 280 calories. Even if you've never had a beer, you'll adore it. You will also probably start smoking after about half an hour – even if you are a lifetime abstainer. You will find you do not need solid food – there is simply no time, what with all those songs you are writing and singing at the same time.

Late at night, as luncheon finishes, you will need a nightcap. Down at the bottom of the menu, you will find an item called Gaelic coffee. Try one – it is a unique prod-uct, particularly if you are a man. You see, in one tiny glass it contains four of the five food groups essential for us to continue our world domination: fat, alcohol, caffeine and sugar. If you are brave and sprinkle salt on it, it's complete – and perfect.

SMILE, DARN YA, SMILE

The quick-service business, in its widest sense, is mature. Depending on your definition, it may be centuries old. It is also broad-based in both content and geography. It ranges from basic techniques that haven't changed since they were conceived to the highest of high-tech processes. In fact, I can only think of two things it lacks: brains (occasionally) and humour (constantly).

Let's take the grey-matter dimension. It was, I think, the glorious P. G. Wodehouse who committed some distant uncle of Bertie Wooster into immortality by describing the shortfall between his ears. If his brain had been made of silk (goes the description) it would 'hardly have sufficed to construct a pair of cami-knickers for a canary'.

Every now and again this industry of ours comes up with an event or episode that parachutes itself right into that league. There's one about at the moment – evidenced by the quick-serve giants deciding that the only way out of the current market stagnation is to discount their flagship products. Just brilliant. It is not sustainable, it is impossible to follow if/when it doesn't work, and fifty years of hard-earned distinctive brand equity is leaking away like a river in flood. The industry has surely learned from its past mistakes – to the extent it looks as though it is managing to repeat them exactly.

Humour – or, rather, the lack of it – is a more subtle omission. I've been a bit daft all my life, but it was a specific restaurant experience that opened my eyes to the potential of humour as a genuine marketing weapon in the foodservice business.

About a decade ago my wife and I landed by accident in a small *trattoria* in Miami. It turned out to be its opening night. It was chaos, with everything going wrong that could go wrong. Being European, we have never considered speed an essential element of dinner, so we told the owner to deal with everybody else and we'd just sit and watch the fun. Much (much) later, he brought a bottle of *grappa* to our table and sat down with us to reflect on his chaotic (but ultimately successful) evening. He asked about our food, and I told him that my *osso bucco* had been fine, but a bit tough – me being of the belief that such dishes need about a day's cooking and then are best served on day three. He paused, then stood up and disappeared back into the kitchen. He reappeared a minute later carrying a drill. I almost fell off my chair laughing. What was more interesting was that we became regular customers.

Has this any relevance for quick-service as against slow-service joints? I think so. During my time on the bridge of the Good Ship Burger King, I found myself in Chicago visiting both franchised and company stores. As ever, the area manager had carefully planned the logistics of the 'tour' and, as ever, I set out to uncover the 'real' business. As we passed the end of a street, I saw one of our signs about halfway down it – and asked to go back and visit. This was definitely not in the plan. It turned out that the store belonged to a franchisee with whom we were in a position of 'antlers locked'. My view on all that was, and remains, simple – the customer doesn't know or want to know who runs the store, but it's under the brand sign, so we should run at the problem, not away from it. We went in.

It was breakfast time, and the sight that greeted us was comical. A long line was waiting at the order point. As each customer was served, they were offered a small ball made out of light foam. They were then asked to have a shot at a small hoop fixed on the menu board behind the counter. If you scored, you got your coffee free. There was all sorts of hootin' and hollerin' going on. The area manager took all this in and turned white-faced, assuming his career had ended. He began to stride towards the store manager, searching his clothes for something that could serve as a machete. I stopped him and asked him to describe what we were seeing. This he did, and we both paused to reflect when he uttered 'happy', 'customers' and 'lots of them' as part of his description. Quite.

What were we witnessing? Was it a wholesale abuse of *that-which-must-not-be-abused* – i.e. the brand specification? Or was it an enlightened attempt to build on a basic successful brand model in an attempt to make it a more personal and memorable customer visit? All I know is that there were more people having a better time in that Burger King than any other we visited.

There is no doubt that the wonderful technological, wealth-creating and social progress of recent history has been accompanied by a whole new raft of stresses and tensions. More people seem to be more miserable than ever. Millions of these stressed folk use a quick-serve restaurant every day. If the industry took on the challenge – collectively and individually – of making them smile once a day, just think of the potential increased customer frequency and loyalty it would engender.

The industry might never have to discount mindlessly again.

A WOMAN'S TOUCH

After a recent visit to South Africa, I was faced with an eleven-hour flight back to Europe. As we took off, I launched myself into Tim Pat Coogan's 700-page biography of Eamon de Valera, the Machiavellian self-server who cast his long shadow over Irish politics for the bulk of the last century.

Somewhere over the Atlas Mountains, while the rest of the plane slept, the book coughed up an astonishing fact. Apparently, de Valera was one of only nine people, acknowledged by Einstein, who genuinely understood the Theory of Relativity. As I looked at the other names, the truth dawned on me – of those listed, only myself and George W. Bush were still alive.

Inspired, I opened another book – and found another list. This one was even more frightening. Apparently, there are also only two people left alive who understand women: me and Jack Nicholson. Now, this one is quite important for quick-serve restaurants in the light of the results of a study published recently on the subject of the effectiveness and efficiency of women as business managers.

One finding of the study will surprise nobody – which is that women, in total, have not achieved equality of either numbers or compensation in management. The second finding might surprise a few – when they do get appointments, women tend to perform better. According to my book, woman outscored men in eleven out of the fifteen management performance categories measured and equalled them in two of the other four.

Of course, it is impossible to generalise about men and women. For one thing, the received wisdom that there are only two sexes is baloney – there must be at least five. There are obviously masculine women and feminine men, many quite happily in public life.

All this confusion tells you that it would be foolish to attempt to draw any conclusions from simplistic stereotyping – so that is precisely what I'm going to do.

On reflection, the findings of the study support what I have long believed but have never before seen quantified. I also believe it has particular relevance for quick-serves.

There are two dimensions of 'management' in this industry where the difference between a masculine and feminine approach can make a difference. First: when you are managing people, you are essentially negotiating an agreement on how you work together. In effect, you are agreeing a charter on how you will relate to each other in the workplace. Now, it's been my observation, in over thirty years in business on both sides of the Atlantic, that most males see a negotiation as a game where there has to be a winner and a loser. Women, on the other hand, move more towards the oriental model where a negotiation is only successful if both parties leave the table smiling.

In a similar vein, the balance between support and control in the management task varies between men and women. Effective and efficient management of people needs the presence of both elements, but getting the balance right is crucial. The masculine approach tends towards making control a priority, whereas the feminine way will seek a better balance of the two. If in doubt, they will lean towards support.

Some will say that these two dimensions – avoiding winning and losing, and balancing support and control – are one and the same. They will say it's all rubbish anyway. They aren't, and it isn't.

I have no idea why these conclusions about the differences in the approach to management might be valid. It may be to do with physiology. It may be to do with traditionally perceived family roles. It may be that we just have to accept there are inexplicable differences between the make-up and approach of the sexes. Frankly the causes do not concern me – and I have neither the desire nor the expertise to go down the road of possible causes. It is my view, however, that differences do exist and are quite widespread. It is also my view that they should be both acknowledged and celebrated.

Time and time again we are made aware of the difficulties in attracting, retaining and motivating staff. At a time when it has become almost universally accepted that front-line people can be key differentiators in the battle to win and retain customers, we continue to pay 'em the minimum we can get away with and treat 'em like dog-doo. It seems to me that these two different approaches have crucial implications when you are talking about recruiting, motivating and keeping a small team of people who deal with your customers every day.

The obvious conclusion is that more women should be appointed to management. The less obvious conclusion is that more of us males should (maybe, occasionally) try a feminine approach.

Excitedly, I look for more 'understanding' lists that I could be on. A-ha! Here's one: a list of people who genuinely understand why Anna Nicole Smith married that ninety-year-old zillionaire. Here we are. Oh, that's not very helpful – there are six billion names on it.

MARRAKECH EXPRESS

Today, we are going to talk about a couple of acres that qualify as the planetary epicentre of quick-service. A-ha! Already I can hear the debate amongst my American readers – with the threat of open warfare breaking out between the supporters of the food court in that huge shopping mall in Minneapolis and that Strip Center in Chicago that has wall-to-wall fast food and seems to go on for miles.

Well, here's the bad news. It's neither – and it's not even in the USA. It is certainly not in the UK or Europe. It is in Marrakech, in Morocco, in north-west Africa.

I've obviously got a soft spot for it – many of you will remember our hit record *Marrakech Express* when I was a member of that enlightened rock band Crosby, Stills, Nash, Young and Gibbons. That aside, it is a gorgeous place to visit. It is a largely Muslim country, but the second thing that hits you as you get off the plane – after the sunshine – is the stupidity of much modern rhetoric and stereotyping. There is no animosity, in fact quite the opposite. Hail a *petit taxi* and ask the fare to your hotel and you will probably get a smile, a shrug, and be told '*Que vous voulez*'. When did that last happen to you in a cab from Heathrow?

On to quick-serve subjects. After living for twelve years in the US, people often ask me what I admire most about the nation and its people. Included in my long list are the happenings in the mid-game break in the Super Bowl. Within twenty minutes, a serious metropolis is built from scratch, illuminated, covered in fireworks and people, sung upon, and then dismantled and completely removed. Impressive, but it is as nothing compared with what happens in the late afternoon in *Place Jemaa el Fna*, a three-acre car-park in the centre of Marrakech.

I have never been sure of the collective noun for quick-serve restaurants – so let's call it a gaggle. From nowhere, as the sun begins to sink, a massive gaggle of QSRs arrives in flat pack form on the back of all sorts of unlikely conveyances (including donkeys). They are assembled, fired up, illuminated, and then thronged (if there is such a word). By midnight, they are all gone. About half the acreage is given to these, and the rest to an eclectic mix of acrobats, snake charmers, street doctors and dentists, fortune tellers, musicians, and loud – and I mean LOUD – drummers. The whole thing – content and process – is astonishing to witness and gets my vote as our planet's quick-serve capital.

Wandering amongst the stalls, it is quickly evident that many of the basic principles of QSRs, as we would understand them, are present. Much of the cooking is with a simple broiler, and much of the hard work and prep is done off-site. They follow the universal quick-serve rule that anything that can't be made into a sandwich can be fried, and sometimes you can do both. Beyond that, there are many differences. Perhaps there are some lessons for us.

Let us first of all get the ugly stuff out of the way. Yes, there are things on display that even I don't want to know about – notably assorted animal heads and varieties of offal. But if we ignore all that, we can start by looking at the provision of drinks. The people being Muslim, the drinks are non-alcoholic, and one side of the whole square is taken up by stalls just pressing fresh oranges. The resultant juice is just gorgeous – and an entirely different animal from the pre-packaged, processed stuff we are generally served in the West. The only alternative drink is hot mint tea, usually served with tiny pastries. The combination is sweet for most Western tastes, but you quickly get used to it. These two simple options make the usual fountain soda, processed juice, and long-dead coffee options of most Western quick-serves seem (at best) uninspired.

They are also big on soup – notably *harira*, which is a meal in itself, containing lamb, lentil and chickpeas. Why don't we make more of soup? It has an almost infinite range of flavours and viscosity and is perfect for the quick-serve process and market need. One problem, of course, is the litany of puerile brand names that have surrounded it in the past – usually involving some version of 'Souper'. It's tough to take anything seriously with that on the store front.

At the core of the Marrakech QSRs is the excitement of blending sweet and sour. The basic soup (above) will be served with honey cakes and dates, and most meals offer some glorious combination of contrasts. *Pastilla* is a startling light pastry pie, filled with pigeon – along with almonds and raisins and then dusted with sugar. Don't knock it till you've tried it.

The big lesson, however, remains the same one I see everywhere else in the world, but which the US – and, increasingly, the UK – consistently ignores. It's about portion size. All the stalls offer affordable fast food, but in every case, the portions are small. There is variety enough to provide for every taste, and enough food available to provide for the biggest appetite. But people graze rather than gorge – there are no bumper portions, no 'two-fers' and no up-sizing.

And here's the bottom line: whether it's a result of the last lesson, or some or all of the others noted above, during a seven-day stay I can't remember seeing a fat Moroccan.

29

I'M ALL EARS

It is generally accepted that communicating and delegating are two of the critical skills needed by any modern business leader – whether the organisation be small, medium, large or American. It is also generally accepted that most people who ascend the leadership ladder need training in both at some stage. I certainly did. I attended a top business school.

Where I lost the plot was when I found out that nothing I learned in business school on those two subjects proved to be of any practical use to me. Most of what I learned about delegation came from soccer – notably when I stopped playing and tried to run a (junior) team from the sidelines. But that's for another day, another chapter. Today I'm going to talk about the source from which I learned most things about effective communication – my father.

He's been passed away for more than a decade now, and I'm still drawing on a full bank of memories. Being from Ireland, born on the banks of the Shannon in Limerick, he could talk the hind legs off a mule. A lot of it was harmless, meandering, charming, user-friendly, poetic, onomatopoeic rubbish – values shared by most Irishmen when they open their mouths and speak. They are also values shared by, in my observation, most pieces of business communication.

The latter, you see, have become the science of *giving out* information – in a controlled, targeted and well-spun way. But that's not what my dad taught me, despite him being a natural at it. He taught me that the more important communication skill, the one that's often forgotten today, is the skill of listening.

I saw him do this a thousand times during our time together on this earth. Somebody would engage him in conversation on a subject about which he knew nothing and he would immediately move into 'super listening' mode, his wonderful green eyes focused intently on the face. You might be talking about the habits of the fresh-water pond toad, about which he knew nothing and cared less, but you would be the only person in his world. Then, as you meandered towards the end of your first sentence, something amazing happened – he would echo your last three words as you said them. He would then end the sentence at exactly the same time as you and nod thoughtfully. You would be amazed and enthralled – at last you had found a fellow pond-toad enthusiast.

This would be repeated several times, and then the two of you would part – he to repeat all of the above with somebody else, probably on the subject of medieval Turkish organ music.

You would move on to a sunnier, happier day.

No effective communication device in history – from smoke signals to e-mail – has been one-dimensional. All of them could or can *receive* information as well as *transmit* it, but the science of modern business communication has all but forgotten that. Today it is all about transmitting: glossy company reports; internal employee newssheets with cool graphics; PowerPoint presentations to analysts, investors, or bankers; e-mails to massive address lists; and media messages to the market. And most managers will acquire skills in public speaking from somewhere. In most big companies, the PR executive is glued to the hip of the CEO.

Of course companies receive information – they research their markets; there are employee suggestion schemes ('If you have ideas, please put them in the Suggestion Box by the reception area ... and don't forget to flush ...'). But very few companies I know are genuinely sound-sensitive – that is, capable of picking up the subtle and sometimes faint messages that come from deep inside what appear to be the homogeneous masses that are your employees and/or markets, and which can prove critical.

Whichever God you believe in (and I'm not going down that road) – and/or the Darwinistic evolutionary process that shaped modern life on earth – gave most of us two eyes, two ears and one mouth. That's four organs to receive information and one to give it out. That's a rule of thumb I've followed all my life in day-to-day business – spend four times as long listening and digesting information as you do spouting off and illustrating vividly that you do not have a monopoly on wisdom.

Why do you think Sam Walton spent so much time in his stores? Of course he was an inspirational figurehead to the troops, and I'm sure he conveyed the shorthand version of Wal-Mart's mission and values. But my guess is that he soaked up feedback like a sponge and never missed a sound or signal that was of any significance.

Listening skills govern your management style. If I visited a region or country in which Burger King operated, it became known I wanted to start the visit as far away as possible from the epicentre of corporate power. When I put my business update on voicemail to everybody each week ('BK Radio', as it became known), I invited everybody to press the reply button and let me know their thoughts. And boy did they ever – but it was wonderful input.

One last thing, however: Doing nothing with the input is actually worse than not listening in the first place. So, the message is not just about listening – it's about listening *and* responding.

The key to this whole communications thing is integrity. As my father practised, and as Tony O'Reilly of Heinz fame once (jokingly!) told me, once you have learned to fake integrity, you're home and hosed.

ME? POSE IN THE NUDE? 30

This chapter started out as a tale of two mayors who have as their fiefdoms two of the world's great cities. It ended up somewhere between a Dixie Chicks anti-establishment tirade and an Alf Garnet-style rant. See if you can figure where I lost the plot.

First, the two mayors: Messrs. Livingstone of London and Bloomberg of New York. Both these guys have introduced controversial legislation that has affected the daily lives of most of their city's inhabitants. Although not directly affecting the quick-serve industry, the legislation was introduced in a way, and with a motive, that suggests that it might become fair game in the future.

Ken Livingstone, a treasured member of Britain's Loony-Left and the elected mayor of London almost by default, introduced a congestion charge (which is now running at £8.00 per vehicle visit) for all vehicles entering the city. There was widespread scepticism from almost all points of the political compass, and we all sat back and eagerly anticipated chaos. Amazingly, it worked like a dream and confounded everybody. City traffic is down by 20%, and average speeds have risen to the fastest in a century. Revenues are being generated to improve public transport, and all we 'I told you so' merchants have gone quiet.

As an example of one man writing his name all over a city's way of life, the parallels with what Mr. Bloomberg has done in the Big Apple struck me immediately. In that city, of course, smoking is now prohibited in all public places, including bars. But it was only when this was expanded to Boston and then Ireland (and now Scotland) that I realised that this, although linked with London's congestion charge in that it also caused controversy, was a different kettle of fish. What is happening here is a prime example of governmental Nannyism, the seemingly infinite desire and ability of those in power to prevent us from harming ourselves.

Let me state upfront: I am a lifetime non-smoker and detest the habit. If and when I stand in front of the Pearly Gates, I will play this card early in my negotiations to get inside – largely because I have few others. Well, no others, actually. But we have to remember that smoking per se is not a sin. In fact, not only is it within the law, it is a legal activity that props up – via taxes – most national economies.

Why, therefore, can we not leave it to the good sense of the citizenry to determine where it does and doesn't take place? If there is a demand for non-smoking bars and restaurants – as I am sure there is – then some owners will make their market distinction on the back of that position, and people will be free to choose. Put one restaurant or bar on each block that is non-smoking, and that's where you will find me.

And guess what: if it's full every night, and the others are empty, then soon there will be two on the block – and so on. This should be no different than some restaurants insisting that men wear a tie. If you are comfortable with that, fine. If not, go someplace else. There's plenty to choose from.

The role of government includes the protection of the governed – but only to a degree and only from predatory or illegal activities. There is a peculiar mentality, however, that seems to invade human bodies as soon as they achieve any governing status – which is that we the People have to be nannied. As I write, the New Labour Government in the UK has just passed its 700th new piece of legislation during its eight years in power.

Nannyism carries direct potential threats for quick-service – one example being that bodies already exist that would like to do away with all 'drive-throughs'. Any business that purveys food that is popular, largely processed, and contains elements of fat, salt and sugar will attract nannies – and, as I have said many times, the industry deserves (and can stand) a lot of criticism for some of its practices. But the key is to get all the information about content and process in the public domain and then let the people choose. Time and again history has shown us that informed free choice is better than regulation.

I'm not really sure whether this confused position of mine is driven by forces from the right of Thatcherism or from the left of Michael Moore. I suppose, however, that to really make my point, I will have to pose, Dixie Chicks-style, naked on the front of a magazine.

You have been warned.

FENCES OF SAUSAGE

Not long ago, Donald Rumsfeld – who looks to me like John Denver might have done had he lived to 120 – aimed both barrels at something he called 'Old Europe'. It sounded intriguing, so I went to find it for you – and to see if there's something inside it called Old European Quick-Service.

Whatever Old Europe is (and I'm not sure Donald would know it if it bit him high on the inner groin), the river Danube is to it what the Mississippi is to the US. Drifting languidly along, it suddenly fools everybody by kicking south and heading for the Black Sea. Twenty kilometres south of this turn, the people from the hilly region on the west bank (*Buda*) decided to link up with the folk from the flat lands on the east of the river (*Pest*). Without, I suspect, paying a penny to 'brand development consultants', they came up with the name Budapest.

It is as 'Old Europe' as it gets, and it had been ten years since I last visited. The place feels wealthier – but it still has many of the old Soviet-style apartment blocks, and there is still the occasional Trabant (the 'East German Porsche') coughing up blue exhaust smoke. Some of the old buildings are stunning – more so when you consider the place was virtually flattened during the Russian advance at the end of the Second World War.

The usual born-in-the-USA quick-serve suspects are now present – Burger King, Macs, and two of the Holy Trinity: Pizza Hut and KFC. The latter two are in one of their joint retail operations and to me look just as uncomfortable together there as they do in Illinois.

Budapest is, of course, the heart of an Old European tradition – 'café society'. If you wander into a *kavehaus*, you are entering into *the* quick-service restaurant of Old Europe. Granted, there is a considerable space-time continuum between there and then and now and the USA, but there are two spectacular differences between the two experiences. The first one is about pace. Budapest is a modern city now, with hustle, bustle, big business, small businesses, government and tourism. However, the difference between eating and drinking in a *kavehaus* and, say, a BK is marked. For those of us who remember records, the difference is like that between 33 rpm and 45 rpm. People slow down in a European café. They look to the experience to charge their batteries, not to drain them some more.

The second big difference is the quality of coffee. There is no excuse – none – for the vapid, vaguely brown liquid served up and described as coffee in most Western-based quick-serves. There are automated bean-to-cup machines available now that can produce an espresso-based drink of reasonable quality both cheaply and quickly. If you served thin mud in Europe, you would close within a week.

Starbucks, of course, tried valiantly to recreate café society. Howard Schultz is on record somewhere as saying he believes Starbucks is more about being a 'third place' (other than the home or the office) than about coffee. Starbucks also brought quality coffee to the mass market. The combination of the two elements represents a fair attempt to turn the *kavehaus* into a quick-serve. Interestingly, it is the only area of explosive quick-service market growth over the past decade in the US and the rest of the West – but it is some distance from the real thing, and the gap is now widening again.

I did find a quick-serve idea that might be transferable to the West – if it wasn't for a tiny obstacle. To give you some idea of where I'm going, if you or I saw a wealthy area, we might say it had streets paved with gold. Not so the *Magyars* of Budapest. They would describe it as having 'Fences made of sausage'. Quite.

Yes, *the* quick-serve idea of the new millennium could be ... the butcher's shop! In Budapest, the ordinary butcher (*hentesaru*) has morphed over time and is now quite a so-phisticated quick-service concept. Every Hungarian eats *kolbasz* (smoked sausage), and there's only one place to eat it – the butcher's. Apart from the refrigerated meats on dis-play for sale, the butcher will have steaming trays and vats containing the day's offerings. There will be a wide vari-ety of sausages, hams and black puddings available, along with bread and mustard. There will also be bowls of pickled cucumbers and peppers marinated in vinegar. You can get snack or main-meal sized portions, and the locals usually arrive carrying a pocket knife. They then carry their meal to a counter and cheerfully begin hacking away. The minor downside to this experience is the spray of paprika grease that targets the front of your shirt.

After experiencing this, I couldn't wait to launch the idea in America. At the back of my mind, I saw this as the New Quick-Serve Thing we've all been waiting for. I would modestly make a few million and then exit stage right – and leave you all to get on with it. Then the snag hit me, and I'm afraid it's insuperable. The idea is stillborn for the USA. You see, there are only three actual butchers' shops left in America – and they are all in China Towns.

Old Europe. New America. *Vive la difference.*

32 MY HIT LIST

I'm in a really bad mood, and it's probably because I've been ill. Being ill to a male over fifty is entirely different in both content and process to what it was thirty years before. In those days, you would shrug off major health threats and traumas as if you were brushing away some mildly irritating insect that had perched on your arm. In my case, I would frequently complete soccer matches minus several limbs and pints of blood, rather like that famous knight in the Monty Python movie. 'Twas as nothing. I would spit at things like the doctor's diagnosis of influenza and head off out into cold, wet, winter nights barefoot and dressed only in a T-shirt.

Today, it has changed. A slight ache or runny nose, and I will take to my bed, often for weeks. I will need potions and tablets by the thousand – and frequently the people at Lemsip have to run an extra shift at their production facilities to keep up.

So, a recent tummy upset floored me. It is only now, when I am just fit enough to take a lightly boiled egg and toast soldiers, that I have diagnosed the source of the problem. I was in a quick-serve recently, and somebody made me a sandwich while wearing plastic gloves. This can't be right, and it must be a major (as yet unidentified) health risk, up there along with SARS, bird flu and MRSA. For all my life I have made sandwiches using my naked hands. When my mum made them for me, so did she, and when my wife has, ditto. Hands are provided for such tasks and, yes, they should be clean before they are so used. If God had meant us to wear plastic gloves when stuffing filling into a bread receptacle, he would have either given us plastic hands to start with or stuck something like a Swiss Army knife on the end of each arm. Plastic gloves are for doctors, for specific male examinations involving a finger and an orifice. They can have no role in or near sandwiches.

Plastic gloves for sandwich making are high on a list of things I am going to ban when I become President of the US or Prime Minister of the UK – I haven't decided yet. In addition, and while I am in this bad mood, let me tell you about some other quick-serve things that tick me off and whose days are numbered after I get the keys to the Oval Office or Number 10:

- Those stupid little sealed packages that contain the essential accessories to quick-serve food – ketchup, salt, pepper etc. These represent the only way you can get any taste or flavour in many offerings and should arrive at the table in a recognisable bottle or cruet set. They should not require a wrestling match and the chipping of your teeth.
- When I first came to the US, for a long time I thought the biggest quick-serve brand was a concept called 'now hiring'. This sign was outside virtually every quick-serve in the US, and that hasn't changed much. You put up this sign, usually with a couple letters missing if it's on a pole, and it tells me all I need to know about you and your restaurant. I go someplace else – where they know how important good staff are, and where they can *find and keep them*.

- If you open for lunch at, say, 11.00 a.m., and you have a salad bar, you can be pretty sure your salad bar will look neat and appetising when you open. By 11.10 a.m., it will look like downtown Baghdad.
- While I'm whining, can I bring up the subject of tomatoes? Not their availability, or even their physical appearance – but what happened to their flavour? I've spent a long time in and around quick-service, but I've never found the (obviously huge) factory where quick-serve tomatoes are painted scarlet and all natural flavour is scientifically removed from them. A quick-serve tomato bears no taste resemblance to the real thing, and I am reluctantly drawn to the conclusion that they must all be strip-mined in Peru somewhere.
- My final act before I am impeached will be to order the removal of all automated hand-driers in men's washrooms throughout the quick-service nation. These are a major health hazard and must go. Here's how it works: your (average) male quick-serve customer, on visiting the bathroom and having completed the activities that drew him there in the first place, will, contrary to female received wisdom, wash his hands. He will then put his hands under the electric drier and start to rub them together under the ensuing flow of hot air. Said flow of hot air will complete the job – if he has two or three days to remain in place under it. He hasn't, of course, so after two or three minutes he abandons his position and exits the bathroom, finishing drying his hands on his jeans. His jeans were last washed two or three months ago. (Note: all this has to be seen in contrast to the French approach to these things – where they wash their hands *before* going to the toilet. Oh, sorry – have I put you off your baguette?)

So, I've a lot to do when I take over – but I do feel a lot better having shared my problems with you. My strength is undoubtedly returning and my temperature is down. Shortly, I may even be able to blow the froth off my medicine.

McD'S AND
THE PERFECT STORM

It is an incorrect assumption, made by most Americans, that all we English live in huge castles and are waited on hand and foot by a livery of butlers and footmen. The truth is a long way away from that. Take my own case, for example: my rather understated home – notice I deliberately stay away from the contentious castle idea – has but fourteen hundred rooms, and the moat is barely 300 metres across at the bridging point. As for a livery of fiefs and servants, I make do with a handful for the essentials – cufflink storage, dandruff management and the like. I make do with an under butler to iron my copy of *The Times* everyday before propping it up on the breakfast tray.

It was the newspaper that jolted me to life yesterday. Yet another hundred column inches were dedicated to the doom and gloom surrounding McDonald's, and the probability that somebody may soon have to switch off the life-support machine. As the only living journalist (and I use the last word in its loosest sense) not to have passed comment on the subject, I thought it was time for me to wade in.

In the movie *Perfect Storm*, a unique set of negative weather conditions come together, and the ensuing freak storm kills George Clooney and his boat. Many are making the argument that something similar is brewing for McD's.

Remembering that McDonald's primary market is to entrepreneurs (who buy franchises and/or invest in partnerships), you can quickly reel off a quorum of freaky-sounding negatives.

- Through its history, the hamburger QSR sector has relied on a momentum-giving goosing every decade or so – a structural development in the offering (e.g. breakfast, drive-through, chicken, value menus, kids' programmes). There hasn't been one for ten to fifteen years.
- For most of its international life, being an American icon brand has put wind in McD's sails. Not any more. Kids in Japan now worship David Beckham, not Michael Jordan. In the Muslim world it's probably wind-against for the foreseeable future.
- The shadow of adverse legal activity has landed firmly on the industry, with predatory consumer lawyers and class-actions on behalf of a fat sedentary nation now on the radar screen.
- In many parts of the world the brand has mature distribution – and further investment can only be defensive and/or cannibalistic.

So, do we prepare the obituaries in advance? Is it all over bar the shouting? Is that a fat lady I hear singing?

What baloney.

Sure, McDonald's have issues, problems and challenges – and they might be on an unprecedented scale – but they also have unrivalled brand-equity, resources and proven skills to bring to bear. What they face is what brand management is all about – it's wildly different in its stages of genesis, adolescence and maturity. They do not need a single revolution, but neither can they do it by just evolution – they need a bit of both. Here are my thoughts.

- They *do* need a goosing, a 'big idea'. They missed the last one (Starbucks). I don't have a solution – and if I did I'd sell it for a squillion dollars. All I know about these things is that they are obvious to the world at large only *after* the event.
- They need some long-term evolutionary programmes – things they need to start now, with ten- to fifteen-year goals. Over time they need to be less American and more worldly; they need to slowly wean their millions of daily customers off big portions; they need more choice *but* fewer menu items (it can be done); they need to listen more to populations worried about their health; and they need to slow down the inside/café offering while speeding up the drive-through.
- The business world – and the McDonald's world within it – needs to evolve to lower return expectations. In many/most parts of the world, low rates of inflation and interest are now the norm, and consistent double-digit percentage rates of return for franchisors, franchisees, stock-holders, vendors and employees – all coming from the same revenue dollar – become anti-gravitational. Greed is the enemy of balance, and balance is what's needed.
- They need to (slowly) reverse the *'Discretion is the enemy of standards'* mantra for the front-line troops.

McD's will disagree with all of the above, of course, and have their own better plans. Whatever. The point is, they should not only survive, but still thrive.

If you all think I'm too optimistic, I should let out a secret – I am a closet fan of McDonald's. You see, in the early 1990s, when we were trying to bring Burger King out of a coma, McD's fired a missile at us, hoping to make our efforts stillborn – they launched the *McRib*. We rushed out to buy one, fearing the worst. With solemn faces, the guys brought one to my table. With suitable gravitas we opened the box. It looked like something that had fallen off an old Russian space station. And you know what – it tasted like something that had fallen off an old Russian space station. They were so kind to me.

Hey, they were kind to me. I can only wish them well.

34
THE ENEMY IS
INSIDE THE GATES

The Austin Powers movie called *The Spy Who Shagged Me* had two effects on me. It amused me, as it did millions of others. It also gave me an enormous shock – or, at least, the title did.

For years, as a Brit living in America, I got away with murder in moments of stress and/or high temper. There were, you see, a few British swear words that were virtually unknown in the US – and you could let fly in company that would otherwise have been seriously offended, and raise no more than a quizzical eyebrow. 'Shag' was one of them, and I remember thinking at the movie's launch that if they ever put that word in lights on the front of cinemas in the UK, my mum would start attacking people with her umbrella.

Spy movies and novels usually have another characteristic that appeals to me. When the plot finally unravels on the next-to-last page, it usually reveals that the real villain has been sitting right next to the President all along – and that he has been a lifetime friend. The enemy has actually been inside the gates. As I read (daily, it seems) about the war the quick-service industry seems to be fighting, I wonder if our real enemies might turn out to be trusted friends who are actually working for the other side.

I have my suspicions about two of our centurions. They have been with us for a long time, and done stalwart service, but they have been acting a bit suspicious recently. Like Jack Ryan, I'm beginning to have my doubts. Let me share them with you.

The first one is the *value engineer*. This is somebody who has been on our side for decades but did his really great work in the '90s. This is the person who can provide any given effect or specification by another method or by using another material – which is always significantly cheaper. Where you used to use wood, he can source recycled tofu to give the same effect. Steel? Pah! He spits at steel. He has come across a new synthetic alloy made from used fertiliser and old cola cans, and nobody can tell the difference. Mayonnaise? Why on earth would you use the real thing when he has found a substitute product that studies have shown cannot be distinguished from the real thing by a focus group of would-be consumers who have been temporarily blinded for the occasion? It is based on bat dung that can be imported for a penny a ton from somewhere in China.

All these alternatives are cheaper by far, and the customer, he insists, will never know the difference.

He is wrong, dear reader. The consumer does know and can tell. And the consumer has seen real value eroded from our industry's offerings on an unprecedented scale in the past fifteen years. The value engineer is part of the problem, not the solution. He is not a friend; he is an enemy.

There's another enemy within our gates – somebody who has been with us from the start, and who we dearly love. He's called *gross margin man*. Most quick-serves (essentially) add value by doing something to a series of products that are bought in and then retailed to a customer in a defined environment. The price you charge for such added value is the point on the graph where the industry attempts to match supply and demand, and is complex to calculate.

There are an almost infinite number of ways you can do it, but to this author's mind there's only one way you can't. The latter, however, just happens to be the received wisdom and prevailing practice in much of the industry – which is to take the bought-in price of each of the products that come in the back door of the restaurant and apply a required margin percentage to each one.

To many in our industry, the individual product gross margin is sacrosanct. It is the one figure that cannot be changed – whatever the circumstances. If sales are soft, there are numerous tactics that can be employed to combat the problem: cut the staffing levels, don't clean the place so often, avoid those irksome maintenance charges, push back the repaint for a year or two, delay investment in that new payroll or till or inventory management system, cut the local advertising, etc., etc. – any or all of those should do it – *but don't question the gross margin percentage* on individual products. Hey, we got 75% in 1975, and that's what the system was built on. Some things can't be questioned; can't be changed.

This guy might just be a bigger threat than value engineer man. My advice would be to be safe. This is a spy movie, right? It's a thriller – PG-15 sort of thing, right? Well, I'd take them outside on to the White House lawn and kill them both, albeit with a silencer.

There may be others – folk actually inside our establishment working against us. I've got my suspicions about *guaranteed return man* and *pay minimum wage at all times man*. You may have your own ideas, but we must fight back quietly for a while, because if they begin to get suspicious that their cover has been blown, our lives will be in danger.

If my magazine column is missing next month, you should fear the worst. But you should carry on the fight.

FIRST IMPRESSIONS

When you reach a certain age – notably mine – you can allow yourself the luxury of looking backwards and regretting: the chances you missed, people you upset, things you wish you had done differently. You can even admit to little personal failings – aspects of your character that, if you had your time again and the benefit of hindsight, you would try to change. In my case, there is one (*Only one? – Ed.*) that has blighted my tramp through life's minefield – I have always been over-governed by first impressions.

My wife has been far more flexible. At our first meeting, at a dance at Liverpool University Students Union in the mid-sixties, she decided there and then that I was either (a) okay or (b) a complete plonker. Approaching forty years later she still hasn't firmed up her view.

I am terrible at this with people. Within seconds of a first meeting – whether it be as unimportant as the lightest social occasion or as important as interviewing somebody for something that might change their life – I make a value judgement about them, and it takes dynamite to blow me away from that position in the future.

It's the same for me with everything, from countries to music, from books to clothes. In February 1963, I was in the

Oasis nightclub in Manchester, England. An unknown rock band were setting up their equipment, but I was far more interested in the girls present. Then somebody called John Lennon hit the first notes of *Twist and Shout* and took the roof off the nightclub. Shortly afterwards, he and his three colleagues were to take the roof off the world. That first impression changed my life.

There are those that think the famous book opening 'Call me Ishmael' is the greatest literary first impression ever. Drivel. Consider this opening sentence from the immortal P. G. Wodehouse:

> *'At the open window of the great library of Blandings Castle, drooping like a wet sock, as was his habit when he had nothing to prop his spine against, the Earl of Emsworth, that amiable and boneheaded peer, stood gazing out over his domain.'*

When you read that, you are hooked. You know what's ahead will be worth its weight in gold.

It's the same with restaurants, including quick-serves.

When you walk through the door of any restaurant, all your senses are on red alert. You are open to any assault of smell, sight, sound, touch, or feel. It is likely that, in the first minutes (maybe seconds) of any visit, one or two of your appropriate senses will register such an assault and it will shape your views about the place. Those views might be positive or negative. They might be nutritional or corrosive, and they might not just last for this visit, but shape a lifetime's attitude. They might not just relate to that single location but might also shape a view about other locations if they exist under the same banner. A whole brand positioning might be affected – all in a few seconds.

It is an enormous opportunity for the enlightened operator. It is in your hands – the ability to affect a fundamental customer attitude to your restaurant, using largely natural (and free) materials, simply by picking a target sense and deliberately trying to affect it positively within ten seconds of somebody – anybody – coming through the door.

But there are pitfalls. Some senses are more easily affected in a positive way than others. Some are hard to affect positively at all, but easy to affect negatively. These I call *dirty window* senses – they respond negatively to things that are bad (dirty windows) but you don't notice them if they are good (clean windows). If your restaurant tables and the floor areas beneath are left cluttered and dirty, it's a huge and early strike against the place for many customers. If it's all clean, it's like a clean window – that's how it should be. Nobody notices.

It is possible, however, to make a strong positive impact within the same timescale. Simple things, like using a customer's first name, can do far more to increase customer frequency and loyalty than discounting and 'two-fers' ever can. And don't believe it can't work for you in a big branded outlet. In one study we did in England, one member of a counter staff remembered 400 customer names!

I'm kinda odd (would you believe?). I'm particularly open to being impressed by the first sounds of a place when I open the door. Does it sound friendly, busy, welcoming? Obviously, however, the main sense that can be assaulted positively for most people is that of sight. What do you see when you open the doors? That might be a welcoming 'meet, seat and greeter', but, if not, you need to monitor what's in the sight line from the door and put something powerfully good in there.

That's the trick. Look at your place. Go outside and walk back in. Pick one sense and have a brainstorming session with your team. What can you do to assault that chosen sense positively in the first ten seconds? It might just be obvious and it might just be cheap. Get it right and it will be highly effective.

As I said, first impressions are critically important to me. I can't wait to see *Basic Instinct II*.

LOVE THINE ENEMY

In an unnerving moment at the end of the 1980s, Mikhail Gorbachev's smiling spokesman, Gennadi Gerasimov, taunted the West with the words, 'We have done the most terrible thing to you that we could possibly have done. We have deprived you of your enemy.'

What rubbish. We have managed to substitute a perfectly adequate new common enemy – and I do not refer to terrorism, the non-Christian world, SARS, AIDS, or any of those lesser ones. I refer, of course, to France.

There are times when I despair of this planet, and this is one of them. Look, I'm a Brit, and we have been at war with the French (on and off) for centuries – the only difference being we now send soccer fans over in buses to flatten their cities. But we still visit, and that's where we differ from the American nation, which has (essentially) pulled up the drawbridge. I love the place, so I'm going to outline a game plan whereby Americans can learn to do the same. It will stop all this 'enemy' nonsense. Right, here goes …

- Visit the place – but not in the way you normally 'visit' Europe. Limit your party to two or four people, and do not stay at a Best Western hotel or a Comfort Inn. These are fine brands, but they are not going to get this job done. Dig into the internet or Fodor's and find a place with a maximum of twenty bedrooms and *phone them up* to fix the deal. Get to know the owners. They will speak English, and you can chat about rooms, facilities and price. You will be friends before you get there.

- Target your location. France is Old Europe. Go to one of its Old Cities – I recommend Nice – and stay in the old part of the Old City (*Vieux Nice*).
- Change your daily biorhythm. Sleep in later, eat later, have a snooze after lunch, and then go to bed later.
- Breakfast is mandatory – but *not* in the hotel. Walk to one of the squares and sit outside – in chairs and tables all facing out into the square. A large *café au lait* accompanied by a *pain au chocolat* will get the job done, and you will find your resting pulse rate dropping into single digits.
- After breakfast you are faced with choices. It's the best time to wander around the flea market, sternly resisting the temptation to spend 145 euros on Napoleon's personal barometer, but soon enough comes the time when you have to choose your meal plan for the day. After breakfast you will need two more meals – an *A meal* and a *B meal*, defined as such by the size, length and alcoholic consumption involved. Many French take their A meal at lunch, but I prefer the lighter one then. In Nice, of course, they invented *salade niçoise*, so that will do nicely – along with a glass (or two) of local *rosé* diluted with some mineral water.
- After a quick afternoon zizz (beach or hotel), it's time to *promenade* – which can be translated as: *walking up and down trying to look thin*. When you are tired, repeat the breakfast formula, only this time with a *pastis*, and sit discussing how fat and ugly the other *touristes* are. This is also where you decide on dinner, which is your A meal.

- Now then, do not choose the dinner venue from your tour guide or any list of restaurant names. Read about the food that's available locally and choose something you can handle that's a bit different than your normal microwaved pap. When you have decided on an item, walk around the squares and look at the menus and the specials until you find it in a restaurant that is: a) busy; b) does not have a 'tourist menu' outside; c) is not over-populated with Germans; and, most important, d) does not have photographs of the dishes posted outside. I'm not being racist about the Germans. To slightly mis-quote Jerry Seinfield, there is, of course, nothing wrong with Germans. But a restaurant that's full of them will not get this job done for you.

- We are coming up to the big finish now. If you have fol-lowed all the above, with plenty of local *vin rouge*, you will now feel French and be enthusiastically defending ridiculous agricultural subsidies and the rights of all male cabinet ministers to have mistresses without in-terference. The last big decision of the day awaits you – what to have as a *digestif* with your coffee. As to the latter, it's mandatory – so don't whinge on about decaf. You'll sleep after this lot, trust me. Now, back to the *digestif* – and I suggest you trumpet your newly discovered Frenchness by upsetting your niçoise hosts by choosing a *Calvados* from Normandy. They'll love you for that.

- When dinner is all over, pay your *addition*, leaving only a 10% tip. Any more and they will think you are mad. Do not smash the plates (that's Greece). Shake hands with your hosts and the occupants of a few nearby ta-bles, and with a cheerful '*A demain, mes amis*' drift off into the warm Mediterranean night, with your woolly sweater tossed casually over your shoulder. Avoid soc-cer fans.

When *demain* arrives, repeat. And repeat and repeat until you must go home.

As you journey back, you can be satisfied that you will have accomplished two things. First, you will have only put on a bit of weight. This is because the French measure it in kilos, and you can't put many of them on in a week. Second, you will have improved world understanding and helped the cause of world peace. And all for the price of a couple of hangovers.

Santé.

ROAD OF LEAST EXPOSURE

After a lifetime of success in the PGA and then on the seniors tour, somebody asked golfer Lee Trevino – as his results started to tail off – if he was considering retiring. As he reflected on a professional life of golf and travel, his reply was: 'Retire from what?'

I feel a bit like that. It's nearly a decade since I made a decision never to be directly involved in big business again … well, to be exact, never to work for anybody ever again. After a quarter of a century of impersonating Road Runner, I set myself some different goals with a different biorhythm – which I'm still pursuing.

One of those goals was to educate myself. This might come as a surprise to some, considering I'd been to school, university and a blue-ribbon business school, and then had countless training and development courses in business. When I had time to pause and reflect, however, I found that all that that had given me was a one-eyed view of real history and a paper-thin, superficial analysis of the world around me. I decided to start again and deliberately built time in my life for the necessary reading, travelling, looking, and listening.

I found out some odd things. In the space of a generation, our approach to the management and acceptance of risk has changed fundamentally. This is true in almost every aspect of life, and particularly so in business. If you had charged a classroom of young executives to come up with two words that captured the spirit of business in 1970, they would have said 'Taking risks'. Now they would come up with 'Avoiding risks'. Today, the business leader's job is to corral half a dozen optional strategies and then pass them to an attorney to make the decision based on what I call the ROLE, or road of least exposure.

This is understandable in a world of ludicrous potential compensation litigation, intense competition, and stock market booms and busts. I guess it's a comforting approach. But, you know what – if you really want to win in your crowded, competitive market, it still won't get the job done. It matters not whether you see your fight as one location against another on the street or at macro-brand level, the ROLE might see you safely in the pack, but it will not see you ahead of it.

Am I advocating rushing out with untried food products or massive investment spends without diligent research? Not in the quick-serve industry, I'm not. But I *am* advocating a step change in a lot of our mindsets. During one of the better historic wars between England and France – the Hundred Years' War – we, the Brits, had the nuclear weapon of the age. It was called the 'longbow' (and you need to read about it to understand how devastating it was). But we lost the war despite this advantage. The reason was odd but has profound relevance to this day. The longbow was a fantastic weapon, *but only to defend*. If you were attacked, it was brilliant, but it was next to useless to attack with – and the derived message is still relevant today. If your mind and resources are geared up just to defending, eventually – eventually – you will lose.

It is all about your state of mind. Winners are not rash or stupid, but their minds are wired more towards the edge of the mental-risk spectrum. That mindset can manifest itself in product range, sales and marketing activity, the look of the place and – perhaps most of all – in the people chosen to work there. These minds obey only two rules: they are prepared to be different and they are prepared to upset a few people to attract a lot.

This last aspect is critical. Today, almost anything you do in business that gets you noticed is likely to upset one faction of the population or another. A lot of business activity is, therefore, neutered of any possible offensive content. The result is that nobody really notices or remembers anything. You personally were probably exposed to thousands of brand sightings or messages yesterday. Can you remember even one? Precisely.

The modern risk-taker understands and accepts that you cannot avoid the risk of upsetting some people if you are to do something out of the ordinary (a.k.a. *distinct* or *memorable*). In fact, if you are not deliberately taking such a risk, your efforts are likely to be stillborn. The risk-taker understands that such a risk can be manageable, and the upside of it is the opportunity to glue in a lot more customers to your concept. Today, frequency and loyalty are far more likely to be achieved by how you do business rather than by what you do.

My re-education exercise has shown me that this isn't new thinking. It has worked in every historic age and in all aspects of society. Rather more surprising, however, is my finding that it is still relevant today and that the advent of a billion lawyers has not made it less so but more so. In addition, my own experience tells me that the modern quick-service business, at all levels, needs it more than most.

For those who are interested, we, the Brits, are still, of course, technically at war with France. The longbow, however, has obviously been superseded by new weapons and tactics. Today, we send soccer fans over. They travel in buses, sing their songs, wipe out a couple of provincial French cities, and are back home for tea.

Now that's effective and efficient.

EVERYTHING CHANGES

I t is rumoured that Nevada has actually sunk by thirteen inches over the past five years on account of the increased per capita weight of visiting tourists.

Now then, it is wise to treat all rumours, printed in books such as this, with a healthy cynicism – and that is particularly so in this case because I have just made that one up on the spot. But a recent visit to Las Vegas, the understatement capital of the planet, highlighted the fact that the *All-American Butt* is expanding fast.

There is an added dimension that also needs considering – that the appropriateness of the Las Vegas tourists' clothing is in inverse proportion to its size. We caught a show by the wonderfully loopy Rita Rudner who explained that Vegas residents (such as her) get anaesthetised to these sights – until one comes into view that simply can't be ignored. At that stage she rushes up to the subject and – in a loud voice – *demands* an explanation.

Yes, today we are going to explore the minefield of obesity and its relation to our quick-serve world – perhaps *the* big gathering storm on our twenty-first century radar screen.

Like all objective contributors to the debate, I should start by declaring my position and biases. My position is that I had a 34″ (86 cm) waist when I got married nearly forty years ago, and I have one today – and it has never changed. My pants have sometimes been tight, sometimes loose, usually OK, but always that size. My weight today is what it was when I played soccer seriously (although its distribution has altered a bit!). My biases reflect my belief that this has been down to a million choices I made over that period – choices to do some things associated with diet, exercise and lifestyle, and not to do others. In short, I drift towards the debate position that if you are fat, it's a result of your decisions. It's not an illness, and you should not point the finger of blame at quick-serves.

I said I 'drift' towards that position. I qualify it by recognising that some obesity – some – is contributed to by external factors. Wealth, for example, clearly helps the cause of the thin. It is difficult to imagine Prince Charles, for example, as he goes about his role of adding zero value to the planet, getting tubby when he is served by personal chefs and footmen. Conversely, if you happen to be one of the few unfortunates who does not have a personal chef, and who adds to this tragedy by not having a home, a job and/or any money, it is likely that you will use any money that might come your way to get something *big* to eat. I can also understand that, living on Planet Stress, as we all do, some folk will seek solace in food as others do in other substances – whether they be in liquid, tablet or powder form, or made from leaves.

So, what's to be done about it? Despite my 'qualifications', I am strongly enough in my debate camp to believe the solution must lie with each individual, and not with macro-level government or industry solutions. I do respect the difficulty that must arise for some extreme cases – but I came across a paragraph in a book recently that might offer a different mental framework within which to address the challenge. The book is called *Quantum Healing*, by Deepak Chopra, and listen to this:

If you could see your body as it really is, you would never see it the same way twice. The skeleton that seems so solid was not there three months ago. Ninety-eight percent of the atoms in your body were not there a year ago. The skin is new every month. You have a new stomach lining every four days ... a new liver every six weeks.

The skin is new every month? I don't know – or care – how true that is (and if it's true, how come the scar on my knee doesn't go away?), but this is the sort of leverage we can use. Here's a way into the challenge if you are seeking to get rid of big poundage. In my view, fad diets are useless, and if you are looking at shifting fifty pounds or more the task must look eternal and hopeless. But supposing you said to yourself, in the mirror, 'Right, the next time my skin comes around, it will not look like this, and, what's more, when my next skeleton arrives, it will look something like this ...' – at which stage you hold a photo of George Clooney or Catherine Zeta Jones up in front of the mirror. Now then, we have a plan. You have time, and you know that you do not have to do all the work – it's all changing anyway, so all you need to do is steer the changes away from business as usual to something different.

How do you steer? If you've given yourself three months, just follow Julia Child's famous advice: *Eat small portions, no snacking, no seconds, and try a bit of everything.* Add to that my own rule when my trousers get tight – no carbs before dinner and alcohol on only two days a week – and I guarantee, when your new skeleton and third new skin appear in three months, everything will be completely different.

I grant you, it will be a wee bit unfortunate if your start position is that of a tubby male and your end position is the Catherine Zeta Jones model, but it's a start and I'm sure you'll cope.

FEEDING PEOPLE?
WHAT'S THE PROBLEM?

I have, of course, run restaurants. I have been involved, as an investor or as a variously ranked employee, with all sorts of different types. From a chain of precisely two Italian restaurants right through to the thousands of Burger Kings which served millions of Whoppers every day while I was captain of that particular ship.

What's different, of course, is that – other than during something called 'executive training' – I have never actually *run my own restaurant*, day in, day out. By that, I mean actually feeding large numbers of people. Occasionally I forget that, and – half-blinded by delusions of competence and grandeur – I decide to do that at home.

Here's how such a day goes, and how and why I get back to my position of safety. Rapidly.

I started the day early, wandering downstairs in my shorts. On the last occasion, my wife and I had stupidly agreed to provide lunch and drinks to a loosely defined group of friends and were not sure whether our invitation included our collective 'children' – all of whom are now between twenty-five and thirty-five years old and still live within striking distance. That causes planning problems, particularly for the bar. Nevertheless, our menu was planned, and – pretty much like Top Cat – I greeted the new day unafraid.

The house looked pretty clean. To me, that is. My wife informed me that it didn't look that way to her, and we would give it a run over before we started setting up. Still in my shorts, I found that the required specification for said 'run over' was that of a SARS ward in Toronto during the recent scare. As a result, I was a sadder and wiser man, smelling of lemon furniture polish, some two hours later. Only ninety minutes remained before the scheduled start.

Here's my next mistake. I lived in Miami for twelve years. If you invited somebody to show up for lunch at 12.30 p.m. in Miami, the well-known northern suburb of Havana, nobody – *nobody* – would appear before 4.00 p.m. This was England, however, and they would all arrive on time. So, I had one hour and a bit to move and sort fifteen chairs, two tables, 150 knives, forks and spoons of various sizes, five sets of thirty plates and dishes and about sixty glasses, and to set up the bar and music. The latter is a crucial responsibility – it's *my* party and I want *my* music. My son can go blow all his 'garage-indie' stuff out of his ear. Whatever it is.

I left myself three minutes to shower and change. I decided, in my wisdom, to wear all black – basically because I need my head examining. This was quickly confirmed. The bell rang spot on 12.30 p.m. and I opened the door to the first guest. It was one of the twenty-five-year-olds – a delightful one at that; the sort you would think might be impressed by my all-black image. 'If it's not Johnny Cash' is the reward I got as she air-kissed her way past me, all smiles, to the bar – a trestle table upon which there were about two dozen uncorked bottles of France's finest export. Depending on whether her friends arrive, this will last all day or ten minutes.

For the record, we served 'nibbles' or 'munchies' first. Halfway through this, a relative arrived, accompanied by three children between three and five. Not part of our plan. Our golden retriever thought this was great fun, and commenced a game of hide and seek. Our SARS-standard home began to look like downtown Baghdad.

I hid in the kitchen, getting the main course(s) ready. I was to carve the ham. With this is mind, my wife had bought me an electric carving knife. Ha! I spit on such convenience. An electric carving knife is right up there with an electric pool cue – it is not a man's way of doing things. About thirty minutes later I surveyed the completed ham plate, which looked as though it was an out-take from *The Texas Chainsaw Massacre*.

We got through to the dessert stage, with dusk setting in. The kids had hijacked the music centre, and something sounded as though a child was in pain. It *was* a child in pain. So much for letting them play with the electric carving knife.

I was partly responsible for desserts. One of the dishes – mine – consisted of tangerines poached in red wine. They had been chilling overnight, but something strange had happened under the foil. They hade morphed from appetising-looking fruit into what I imagine a malignant external growth on the Elephant Man might look like. Everybody studiously ignored them and headed for my wife's ice cream creation.

Well into the night, the surviving bodies decided to play a game of Trivial Pursuit. We decided that the men would play the women, but complicate this already dangerous approach by having a sub-plot whereby the young played the old – rather like Spock and his multidimensional chess. Absolute chaos ensued, and bits of the cheese course started flying.

About 10.30 p.m., the 'youngsters' decided to walk up to the pub for the last round, and steadfastly refused our company. An hour later, they arrived back – and with what? Oh, goody, a bottle of Bushmills Irish whiskey. That's whiskey with an 'e' in it. Not that it made a big difference. At 12.30 a.m., just twelve hours after the opening bell rang, the last guest left. Three hundred and twenty-nine tables, 3,762 chairs, 43,765 pieces of cutlery, 65,983 glasses, and 72,876 empty bottles were jammed in the dishwasher. I discarded my Johnny Cash outfit. Armed, once again, only with my shorts, I retired.

No, gentle reader, I haven't 'run' restaurants, and it shows. Gentlemen and ladies of quick-service, who do it every day, I salute you.

40 NEXT TIME YOU POST A LETTER ...

A while back, McDonald's dropped Kobe Bryant from its sponsorship activities, and the news broke like a thunderclap in England. Everywhere I went, people crowded me, pushed microphones into my face and generally harassed me – always wanting to know the answer to the same question: 'What is a Kobe Bryant?'

I had to explain to them, of course, that it is not a 'what' but a 'he' – and he is someone who is seventeen feet tall and who plays NBA basketball in America. I then have to explain the NBA, which I do as follows: five *very* tall men run up a wooden court and (usually) score points by throwing a ball through a high hooped net. Five different *very, very* tall men then run up the other end and (usually) do the same. This progresses until about fifty seconds before the end of the game when, by some strange freak of the space-time continuum of the kind written about by Stephen Hawking, those fifty seconds last just over an hour, and then one side wins.

Back to sponsorship – and the question that bugs me yet again as I look at a paper in front of me telling the world that Vodafone has just canned its sponsorship deal with Manchester United (the world's biggest soccer 'brand'). Why do sane businessmen and women continue to flush *huge* sums of money down the pan by pursuing this odd mix of science and art? Marketing gurus are often in favour, arguing that – if you take the five-point marketing cycle as: 1) generating awareness of your product or service; 2) securing a trial purchase; 3) getting a repeat purchase; 4) encouraging increased frequency; and, finally, 5) landing that Holy Grail called customer loyalty – then effective sponsorship budgets can help any or *all* of those stages. What pish.

Here's my position. If you are running *any* quick-serve business, and you receive a sponsorship proposal, you should consider it carefully. You should sleep on it, walk the dog and think about it, talk to your partner about it, phone a friend about it and then sleep on it again. *And then politely turn it down.*

It is not the best way to spend your hard-earned marketing support money. Markets are so cluttered and competitive today that you need to get customers to change behaviour when you get a message through to them – not just change an attitude or perception. Billions of dollars go into sponsorships annually, and I do not understand how the big spenders figure it actually works, let alone how it justifies itself. Take one high-profile programme, for example. The US Postal Service sponsored Lance Armstrong and his team – who have triumphed an unbelievable seven times in the Tour de France. Now here's the problem: only about fifteen Americans know that the Tour de France is about bicycles and is the world's greatest bike race. Of those fifteen, only three still write to other people, and they don't have a lot of options when they post a letter in the US.

If it doesn't fly in the US, does it work over there? Over in France, *Le Tour* is an annual sporting highlight for millions of Europeans. Armstrong's victories have, as a result, given him megastar status. So, is this where the sponsorship pays off? When these millions visit the US next time, is the plan that they are suddenly resolute in their determination to seek out *only* the US Postal Service when they want to post a letter home? Er, as against what other option?

I am confident I know the determining drive behind most sponsorships. It is the chairman (it doesn't happen with chairwomen) who trousers a huge chunk of the advertising budget and decides that the brand will lend its name to (let's say) a PGA golf tournament. Is this driven by target marketing? No, it is not. It is driven by enabling him to: a) play one of the world's best courses in the lead-off pro-am with Tiger Woods; b) watch the happenings on the eighteenth hole from twenty feet away with a martini in hand while playing King-of-the-Tent; and c) go on TV in his Ralph Lauren blazer and polo shirt and offer his golf wisdom in a thirty second slot at the end. Is that cool, or what? And it's bound to make the target audience feel warm and attracted, isn't it? Isn't it? I said *isn't it?* Yeah, right. Who cares?

Look, I'm not saying sponsorships can't add value. Nike morphed from being a US sneaker-marketer to being a global sports equipment and apparel supplier on the back of extensive and risky marketing programmes that included clever sponsorships in golf (Tiger) and soccer (Brazil, Manchester United, et al.). All I am saying is that, apart from the obvious risks of associating your brand with somebody who might end up facing a judge, the huge relative amounts of money required to sponsor anything or anybody of note are not likely to be the best way to spend your quick-serve brand support money – whether that be at national brand level or that of a single owner-operator. If you are insistent, I would limit it to the *very* big (e.g. Nike-type) or the *very* small (e.g. local junior baseball-type). In the middle, it just gets lost. Remember: you need to change consumer behaviour when you spend – 'feel-good' stuff doesn't cut it anymore.

If, however, after all that, you remain determined to spend your money in this way, I have an opportunity for you. I am hoping to represent my country in the 2008 Olympics in the KFC Bucket Leap competition – but a shortage of funds is limiting my altitude training. You know where to find me, and all cheques will be welcome.

THE RISING SUN

Japan came to the top of my mind recently. Having breakfasted on news of the appointment of an ex-Apple executive to help McDonald's' Japanese operations to get out of the fairway bunker they've landed in, I found myself hosting our eldest son (aged thirty) to a sushi lunch. The meal came by in tiny individual portions, on small plates, via a sort of model railway, and was memorable for two things. First, I confirmed my love of the food – which is strange considering that a decade or so ago I used to put similar looking delicacies on the end of my fishing hook. Second, the bill was totalled by the simple method of adding up the number of empty plates on your table. You couldn't see my son behind his pile, and the bill came to roughly the equivalent of the GDP of a mid-sized Scandinavian country.

I have spent a lot of my life exposed to varying Japanese images and influences. The first should have been strongly negative, but oddly became the opposite. My father was a Japanese prisoner of war and suffered horribly – and that should have been enough to instil a lifelong hatred of all things Nippon. That it didn't was a mark of my father's spiritual strength. He rarely spoke about his experience, but when he did it was to make the point that the Japanese simply had no idea how to handle POWs. In their culture, if you lost at war, you died – and they simply had no concept of what to do with thousands of prisoners. It reined in my horror enough for me to keep some sort of open mind.

At university in England, one of my buddies came from Tokyo. Everything appeared to be normal until the first vacation, when he told me he was staying in the country to work on his English. He then told me that his grandfather, who ran the family, had decreed that it was too cold to send his wife over to join him, so the family was sending *his mistress instead*. As you do. When I visited him some years later in Tokyo, this 'sharing' situation was still in place, and I suggested to my wife it might be something we could think about back in England. The scar still exists where she hit me with her Chelsea Flower Show programme.

I landed in Japan for the first time in 1978 – leading a team buying an automated warehouse system for a big brewery. My questioning fascination began to turn to genuine affection. Their whole national logic is different to ours on many planes. When I pointed out that our system would need more safety protection in case somebody broke into it and got injured, they looked at me as though I was mad. Their thinking was simple – if a burglar broke into a place, he deserved to be chewed up.

My '70s trip was also responsible for one of the funniest scenes of my life. One of our mechanics got terribly (no polite way of putting this) constipated. It was an all-male party, and the rest of us were, to put it mildly, not very helpful. But we did convince him to go to the pharmacy in the basement of our hotel. Three of us then watched the scene hidden behind a big stack of shampoos, and I have to tell you that if you have never seen a male, English mechanic try to explain to a female, non-English-speaking Japanese pharmacy assistant the problems of constipation – *in sign language* – you have not lived.

I have been back to the islands several times and continued to digest the complexities of this beguiling nation. My wife became involved in Ikebana – floral art – and I became aware that simplicity, minimalism and clarity could also bring power and beauty. My business education had tended to indicate the opposite.

I'm not sure I could advise anybody about Japan. If your quick-serve brand is not in the country, should you enter the market? If you are in it, what are your prospects? After all my exposure, if you ask me those two questions, all I can do is echo Mayor Giuliani's words after 9/11. This is what I know and this is what I don't know:

- In Japan, whatever corporate architecture is involved, they will do it their way. They will work to their charter, their rules and their code. Their position will be thought through and will be based on a mix of indefatigable logic and unanswerable heritage. If it doesn't match yours, they will be polite but not move an inch.

- Their economy is not out of the woods yet. Mr. Koizumi's government was strong on promise, but has not delivered. He remains too cavalier with public spending, but there are two pieces of good news worth banking. First, over the past decade, the Japanese economy has gone through as near a revolution as it has ever experienced, and their institutions, attitudes and executives are now in better shape to face changing global challenges. Second, many forecasts are now predicting a period of steady growth for their economy – unexciting, but highly welcome after the woes of the past ten years.

- They will remain uninterested in short-termism. It will still be the nature of the beast to identify a game-plan and then stay with it for the long term.

- Despite all the changes, their business fundamentals will still be built from a different DNA than ours in the West. If you want to do business there, the rule is still to find a local partner.

Just as the Eskimos have fifty different words for snow, the Japanese are rumoured to have fifty different words for a Walkman. Owing to the average height of their men, however, their language has no word for slam dunk. Can you believe that?

Neither can I.

42 O SOLE MIO

The sun rises over the Bay of Naples, and the water winks its reflection at me. Despite four espressos, I struggle to translate the local morning paper, *Il Mattino*, into English. In the distance, the ghostly peak of Vesuvius seems to echo the whole environment's laughter at my pathetic efforts.

Suddenly, one paragraph seems to make sense, but I can't believe my translation. For the first time since I arrived, I break into a brisk walk and get myself an English language paper. My fears are confirmed: Shell, the imperious global oil giant, has joined Enron, Parmalat, World-Com (et al.) on the list of corporate evil-doers. It appears the company has not only over-stated its oil reserves by an astonishing 25–30%, but also knowingly done so. There's a blame-storming session going on, they've already zipped shut a few body-bags (including one on the chairman), and the lawyers on both sides of the case are looking forward to years of gainful employment. This one stuns me particularly, and there's a personal reason.

Around the end of my second decade as a human, I was in a mess. I was a rebel without a clue, heading for a lifetime of serial trouble and underachievement. Suddenly, I got a number of breaks that changed everything for me.

One of those was a junior job with Shell in England. My dad thought I had won life's lottery, and it is difficult to describe credibly today what it was like to land a job with Shell in the UK nearly forty years ago. It was almost like joining the Church. Once you'd got in, you didn't leave – and the average week was spotted with visits to the canteen to present somebody with a twenty-five, thirty or even forty-year service award. The company watched me through university and then paid (full salary plus fees) for me to go to one of England's premier business schools.

I then signalled that I was part of the generational paradigm shift in the relationships between corporations and their employees by saying 'thank you for all that', by being headhunted and joining another company. Shell survived this potentially mortal blow and carried on as before: a bit top-heavy, a bit bureaucratic, somewhat paternalistic, genuinely global, astoundingly capital-intensive, a tad conservative – and stinking of integrity. If in doubt, three things always ruled: integrity, *integrity* and **integrity**.

There is no doubt I owe Shell much. When I hear present-day CEOs mouthing off the shallow lie that their 'people are their greatest asset' I feel like upchucking – quite simply because I have always believed that was for real, and I was taught it in a company that was all about technology. What has happened to Shell is beyond belief to me. I wonder just what will I feel when I pull up under that brand sign next time? Will I link the guy behind the register, or the product quality, with the deceit and malice aforethought that seems to have been *de rigueur* in the boardroom? I tell you: it will be hard not to.

Here's the spill-over for quick-service. I have contended for some time that the art of getting distinction in cluttered, competitive markets (a.k.a. branding) has ceased to be just about what you do. For decades (centuries, perhaps) the specification of your product and/or service was enough to get you market distinction. But now there is another dimension in play. The values you espouse as a company are becoming critical differentiators – and customer loyalty is recognising your corporate personality as well as its product portfolio. Companies who understand this, and get their game-plan right, seem to punch well above their marketing-spend weight.

Virgin does this brilliantly. The company constantly pushes its corporate personality attributes (value, fun, innovation) out into space whenever it gets the chance, either through formal marketing or PR and photo opportunities. Trust me, this is a science, not an art form, and it seems that people who are comfortable with these values are then more inclined to try the products/services with the brand name written on them. Think about Apple, Benetton, Tesco, RyanAir and Haagen Dazs – they all stand for different values, but are all quite clear in what they are.

Let's bring this closer to home. I don't care whether you are CEO of a quick-serve giant, or the operator of a single location. Mentally, walk outside your store or your brand, and look back. You see the brand sign. Now, forget about your product for a minute. What signal does the brand sign give off about *how* you do business? What does it say about what you stand for? Try a Virgin analysis: limit yourself to two or three words. Then, and here's where the fun comes in, check your results with some of the folk who buy your products – but I suggest you have a strong gin and tonic first.

It's cool to take this one step further. Forget your business and concentrate on yourself as a leader. If you have anybody reporting to you directly, try the same exercise. If you were in a group of your first-line reports, and you walked in the room, what would be the consensus view of the values you exude? What do you think your people think you stand for? Hey, if your people are your greatest asset, it's kinda important, yes? You might want to check your results out again, with them this time. But be *really* careful with this one – it can go wrong.

Writing this stuff is exhausting, and I've moved from espresso to grappa. At least, I think it's grappa. It is only when I look at the label on the latter that I realise I have made another translation mistake from the Italian. I should not have drunk it. I should have dabbed it behind my ears.

Ciao.

43

THE LONG RUN

Anytime now a number of the global quick-serve brands celebrate a half century of existence. That's cool, and a matter for some pride, but in the gene pool of longevity, they are splashing about in the shallow end.

Back in 1548 (the same year my beloved Manchester City Football Club won their last silverware), Nostradamus foretold of a future historic business combination:

From Albion's shore shall come a marvellous conveyance, a carriage silincieux bearing the arms of Rolles de Roi.

Is that spooky, or what?

You can choose to believe it as a prophecy or not, but some three and a half centuries after he penned those words, and exactly a hundred years ago, Frederick Rolls and Henry Royce met in England and gave birth to a company whose name has become familiar in every country – and synonymous with excellence. At Burger King, we called the Whopper the Rolls Royce of sandwiches. I don't own a Rolls Royce car, but I find something comforting about seeing the R-R logo on the engine of any jumbo I'm on. A century from now, who knows how we will be travelling, but I suspect R-R will be written on the quality end of it.

This longevity thing is not just about big brand names. The fourth-century BC Chinese belief that the world is made up of opposing forces has been reflected in their cooking ever since then. The notion of balancing such forces is central to the famous Sichuan cuisine – in this case six of them (*ma*, *la*, *tian*, *suan*, *xian* and *ku* – spicy huajiao, hot peppers, sweet, sour, salty and bitter respectively). That's a way of life – and a way of eating – that has survived for more than two millennia. Again, you get the feeling that, two more thousand years from now, assuming our assorted gods spare us, the same principles will still be in place.

A while back, I meandered around the ruins of Pompeii. Beforehand, my knowledge of the place (and the events) was limited to distant school history lessons, a few TV shows and Hollywood sound bites. Walking the streets of the place brought home to me – just as so many things do today – just how little I know and appreciate about our planet and its history. Pompeii was a town of some 60,000 inhabitants, nestling under Mount Vesuvius. Nobody even suspected the latter was a volcano until 24 August AD 79 when it erupted, covering the town in mud and ashes. The fantastically preserved domestic, commercial and community buildings (still not all excavated) reflect a metropolis of advanced culture and bustling business activity. Social developments were illustrated by a 20,000-seater sports amphitheatre, extensive graffiti and about seventy quick-serve restaurants.

The latter fascinated me. They are quite different from the many *tavernas* that are also evident in the preserved ruins in that they are *counter-service*, with the counters housing several fire-holes for preparing hot food. I spent an hour or two finding out what I could (and imagining the rest) of a typical lunch menu from the first century AD. The area is well south of Europe's Olive Line, and olives (and olive oil) would join the grape (i.e. wine) as a mainstay. The hills of Campania would provide good grazing for livestock and rich wines. They had salt (via solar evaporation), and so could keep hams and cheese. They had vinegar. They made sausages from pork and other meats, preserved in salt, seasoned, and stuffed into natural casings from intestines. They had greens, including fennel, asparagus and cabbage. Indeed, the origin of the word salad comes from the Latin for salted greens. The Mediterranean was full of fish, ranging in size from anchovy to tuna, and commercial boats would trade all of the above for salt cod from the north Atlantic and spices from the Middle East – and even further afield. Bread would be a source of carbohydrate.

All this research made me *really* hungry, so I ambled into an *osteria* in the square in Sorrento. I ordered a plate of local olives and a carafe of local wine. I then had a plate of mixed, fried (small) local fish and finished off with some local ham and cheese. The sun combined with all these ingredients, and I headed off back to the cool of my hotel room for a well-deserved nap. As I closed my eyes, my thoughts were that I had replicated – exactly – a meal that somebody could have been eating 1,930 years ago when their peace was interrupted by a noise. And I mean a *noise*.

Some things are timeless, and a lot of people quite like that. If I'm in Miami, I head for the Versailles restaurant, or the Captain's Tavern down south. In Chicago, it's Melman's Scuzzi; in New York, it's Madhur Jaffrey's Dhavut; in London, it's Joe Allen's or Langan's. They've all been around a long, long time. They are built on strong foundations, and a lot of people like that, including me.

There's so much uncertainty, so much tension and so much technological change going on in our world that it's almost nonsensical to try to forecast the future. But here's a test for any quick-service. Spend five minutes with a piece of paper and write down five *big* things you think are going to happen in the next twenty-five years. Then try to picture what the place you are thinking about *might* look like against that background. It might, just might, help some short-term decisions you were planning to take anyway.

Then follow the rest of my advice: finish your wine and go for a nap.

I'LL TAKE THE HIGH ROAD

Normally, about this time of year, I seek some peace and quiet for a period of private reflection. I take this very seriously, and I am often to be found in a cave in the foothills of the Atlas Mountains in Morocco, eating only locusts for a couple of weeks while I think about eternity. And if you believe that, you really do have to get out more.

This year, by way of a change, I decide to fly into Cape Town to see how many line-fish I can eat at one sitting in a neat little café in the V&A Waterfront.

The trip is full of surprises from the outset, starting on the long plane journey to South Africa. Like many guys, modesty is not my strong point. In fact, if they ever put self-delusion in the Olympics, I would be a shoo-in for gold. Suddenly, however, I decide that I am rather pretty, of all things. The prime reason for this revelation is that I share the overnight flight with the Irish rugby team, who are flying in for a series of internationals. I know from experience that nobody looks their best as they get off a plane after an overnighter, but these guys are something else when it comes to being ugly. I also realise why American men wear crash helmets for (gridiron) football – it helps to keep your nose somewhere near the middle of your face. There was not one nose in the Irish team where it should be, and not one ear that reflected the shape that God intended. It takes a lot to make me look pretty, but there you go.

The trip from the airport into Cape Town reminds everybody of the contrasts of this staggeringly beautiful but still troubled country. As the glorious backdrop of Table Mountain slowly reveals the high-rise wealth of the city and the showy waterfront developments, your car takes ten minutes to pass the first township and its horrendous quality of life. The history of the country is built on such contrasts – extreme poverty and wealth, danger and refuge – and the questionable best and profound worst of imperialism. South Africa is, of course, home of some of the earliest human settlements, where groups of twenty to eighty hunter-gatherers lived together for security. A bit like Miami's gated communities, really.

It is now more than a decade since democracy finally won out, and that anniversary triggered Nelson Mandela's final, *final* retirement. This guy fascinates me. To be brutally honest, I knew very little about him during his long incarceration on Robben Island. In our world, one man's terrorist is another man's freedom fighter, and much of how we judge these things depends on the media we are exposed to – in other words, it depends on Rupert Murdoch's chosen position on the subject. But as I got to know enough to form my own judgement, it became clear that the latter part of the last century had produced one of history's *special people*.

Mandela is not a saint. His eye for the ladies and his refusal to mince words or tolerate fools would make him an uneasy fit in most American corporations. But his challenge was not to support the market capitalisation of some shadowy global enterprise, it was to lead and steer his country through a profound transition at a speed that was simply unprecedented. Almost every commentator forecast civil war and bloodshed. It never happened – and, more than a decade later, there is a lot of stability and optimism, and a realistic understanding of the residual problems.

Mandela has much to teach us in business. (There you are, see? You knew I'd get round to it eventually.) Over a career, many of us will face business crises. All the options for the next steps will seem ugly. The sheer size of the task will appear insuperable. Pause for a minute, and imagine your worst-case business scenario, then multiply it by a million to get some idea of what this guy faced. And then pause a bit more and register this: *he made it through, and he got there without abandoning the high road.* At every point, where it must have appeared easier to resort to violence and extremism, and for him to morph into (yet another) dictatorial warlord, he chose to have faith in the core human spirit and to try and get minds to meet other minds rather than bullets to meet skin. There is an old saying: *It is crucial to talk to your enemies. Otherwise, you only talk to people who agree with you.* Did he ever. The world would be a different place if a new Mandela could suddenly appear on the cast list for the Middle East or the Korean Peninsula.

Quick-service is always in transition – whether it be a single owner-operated location or a global giant – and in transition there are always potential winners and losers. Transitions can be managed for the better, but in the West we believe that has to be about winning and losing. The idea that a better – more sustainable – transition might emerge if you leave something on the table, and other parties also gain something, is alien to us. You might want to give it a thought. Take the high road.

Meanwhile, as ever, here are some practical tips on South African cuisine. Eat anything out of the cold ocean or the big powerful rivers: snook, line-fish, kingklip or shrimp. While you are doing this, make a note of my view that fried fish does *not* belong in a hamburger bun.

While in South Africa, do not – and I offer this from personal experience, the details of which would provide you with just too much information – attempt to eat anything with ostrich in it.

OH, WON'T YOU STAY?

My initial position was to stay quiet when asked about the continuing revolving door on my old CEO's office at Burger King. There were two reasons for my silence. First, I left that stage long ago and have neither the wish nor the information necessary to comment specifically or wisely. The second reason is also simple: There are some things better left unsaid. Oh, how I wish everybody had such sense.

As ever, however, my initial position weakened and has now broken. As it normally does, this happened at a party when I was trapped in a corner by a hard-bodied supermodel, who would not release her trapping leg until I had outlined my thoughts on CEO tenure. Yes, I know I am making this up, but it's my book.

Where was I? Oh, yes: CEOs and how long they should stay in position. Let me first put *my* record straight. I stayed in Burger King as CEO for five years, in the early 1990s, after initially agreeing to a three-year contract. In the decade before my arrival, there had been 1,378 CEOs, some of them lasting as long as four days. Since I left, there have been, by my calculation, another 2,722, with the range of tenure stretching from seven minutes to well over a week.

So, is this CEO-churn a bad thing? The world can make its own mind up about BK; I'm going to widen the debate to business generally. I have here, before me, an official statement from the revered IBO (the Institute of the Bleeding Obvious): *Of course it is dumb business to change your CEO every time Wogan appears on the TV.* The blindingly obvious prime reason is that it gives off clear signals to all stakeholders that the business is in trouble. On receiving these signals, it is unlikely that these stakeholders will seek to increase their stake in the business (whether that stake is an investment, a supply position or an employment contract). At best they are likely to assume a holding pattern for their stake; at the worst, they may seek to exit.

CEO-churn also inhibits the implementation of deepset strategic change. Of course, there will be changes with each new CEO: he or she immediately wants a new advertising agency and a gaggle of new key executives; product development priorities will alter; the company will exit a few markets, and enter others; R&D spend will go up, or down; there will be a new raft of policies, ranging from corporate travel allowances to diversity training; everything that was blue will become green; and so on and so on. In short: a load of tinkering goes on, which then all changes again when the next CEO arrives.

For most companies, however, this sort of change is not enough. These programmes are about *doing things differently* – but there also needs to be a programme to contemplate *doing different things.* These are changes to the fundamentals of the business – and they can take years to design, test, implement and tweak. Quick-service needs long-term change programmes on portion size, menu range, health positioning, internationalism, price-pointing and wealth creation. These are what I call deep-water policies, and you can't get out there at them if you are constantly splashing about in the shallow end. They need time – but more than that, they need continuity of thought. They need the benefits that come from the same folk designing them, implementing them, and then *being held accountable for them*.

Is there no case for changing a CEO after a year? Of course there is. If it's clear that the CEO isn't a fit – and you never *really* know until they are behind the desk – a great way of turning a non-fatal mistake into a mortal failure is to do nothing. But that's quite different to knee-jerking just because some twenty-year-old Wall Street analyst fires a broadside about short-term profits or a group of investors or franchisees has a communal whinge.

Now then, let's come at this from the other end. Can a CEO stay in position for too long? Oh, yes. Indeedy-doody. History will look back on Margaret Thatcher and Ronnie Reagan quite differently. Reagan rode off into the sunset after his two terms in office to the sound of applause – loud from his political think-alikes but also quite warm from his political foes. In the cycle of political life, his heritage was that he was conservative against the backdrop of a conservative *zeitgeist*, and he did what he felt he had to do. He was doctrinal but a good communicator. All that, and more, could be said of early Thatcher. It is my belief that if she had left power after eight years, her heritage would be as favourable as Reagan's, if not more so. In reality, she stayed on. And on and on. It all went pear-shaped, and she ended up being thrown out by her own party, and her heritage is a cross between Lady Macbeth and mad cow disease.

You can stay too long. I felt it after five years in BK. People start to anticipate your thinking and tell you what you want to hear. Try as you might, you get detached from the short-sword fighting. You repeat yourself and run out of ideas. You get comfortable. You lose the plot.

The Founding Fathers had it right – a maximum of two terms of four years. What they didn't know was that they had invented a formula for CEOs as well as Presidents.

As I finish talking, I notice the eyes of my (trapping) supermodel have glazed over. She makes no attempt to stop me as I squeeze by. I decide I will get us another drink, and come back and tell her my views on corporate re-engineering.

She'll like that.

LONDON CALLING

As many of you know, part of my England-based portfolio of duties is to advise Queen Elizabeth. She and I call them our 'Strategy and Vision Sessions', and we normally meet, on the last Thursday of each month, in a Starbucks in London's West End. I can't tell you which one – if I did, I would have to kill you for security reasons – but, for those of you who like to know whatever details you can, I can reveal that she usually has a double tall skinny latte (with a ginger biscuit for dunking – which she does ever so daintily).

Our agenda tends to be about global issues, but last week she, rather nervously, pinned it right down to a London problem. There is, apparently, a shortage of American visitors here – the result of a combination of the US dollar's weakness and general 'security' scares associated with international travelling. She wants me to use this chapter to try to sell Americans the idea of a visit to this fine city, with the prime aim of spending some dollars.

The obvious place to start when listing London's attractions is with our Black Cabbies. Black is the colour of the cabs, not the drivers, who are of every ethnic hue imaginable, and they are absolutely brilliant. London's city street system is twenty times more complex than New York's, but you simply cannot catch our cabbies out. They train for years to get *The Knowledge* before they can qualify as a taxi driver, and they know every tiny street and alleyway. The only downside arrives if and when you drop a hint that you enjoy conversation. Within minutes you will be pinned back in your seat (metaphorically) while you go through his (or her) recent divorce, back problems, children's progress at school, ageing parent's ailments, and soccer team's dire performance. If it's summer, substitute cricket for soccer.

What else? Our one and only Royal Family, of course. Since Diana's death, when we learned to be emotionally incontinent like the rest of the world, the Royals have given us enormous entertainment and provide perpetual highlights for any tourist visit. Charles and Camilla out-do anything from the scriptwriters of *Sex and the City*. Our tabloid press, unreadable for anything newsworthy, track this wondrous family of dysfunctional invertebrates on a regular basis, and there is invariably a weekly 'butler's confession' or 'love rat exposure' to keep you entertained in the rain.

Ooops! I shouldn't have mentioned the rain.

Are you worried about security? Forget it. We've got it pinned down. Here's a true story. A while back I had a ticket to watch England play cricket at Lord's, the home of the game. The tradition is that, on the Saturday, you take a picnic, albeit one with a heavy liquid bias. It was my turn to provide lunch for my pal and I, and I arrived with my cool-bag well stocked. To my horror, there was a security search at the gate. And, as my bag contained a glass bottle of claret, assorted knives and bottle openers, glasses for imbibing, and sandwiches wrapped in foil that suddenly looked like Semtex, I thought I would lose the lot. The security guard opened my bag, delicately took everything out, and then delicately put everything back in and waved me in. Having just flown out of the Dallas/Fort Worth Airport, where I was asked to 'voluntarily' take my shoes and belt off at the security checkpoint, I didn't understand why I wasn't being ushered off to jail. So I asked him what he was looking for. 'Hooters and whistles' is what he told me, without a word of a lie. In England, we can carry weapons that could potentially kill, hijack, and blow places up, but we cannot hoot and whistle at a cricket match.

Now then – food: so important to we quick-service folk. A great deal of unfair *rubbish* is talked about British food. I am, therefore, simply going to give you details of a couple of mouth-watering British recipes that are available in most good restaurants, and let you be the judge. Here goes:

- **Guinness and haggis:** Take six pints of Guinness (a black Irish beer) and one haggis (sheep's offal and organs wrapped in its stomach). Prepare a pan of boiling water. Drink the six pints of Guinness. Then throw the haggis away.
- **Bang-bang chicken:** Take a three-pound, organic, free-range chicken and pre-heat the oven to 240 degrees. Remove the giblets and stuff the chicken with uncooked popcorn. Put the chicken in the oven, and in fifteen minutes there will be a 'bang-bang!' and the chicken will *fly* – through the oven door, to your table.

How can you resist those? You must believe me, our cuisine is the highlight of any tourist visit to our lovely island. Only recently, an American friend of mine was recounting his experience as he sought food in a pub in Covent Garden, the epicentre of London's tourist activity. Not recognising any of the dishes in the glass-covered serving counter, he was going to ask the barman's advice when he saw a sign behind the bar. It said: 'A pie, a pint and a friendly word'. Well, reassured by this helpful guidance, my friend ordered a pie and a pint of beer. When they were delivered, before taking it all back to his table, he leant across the bar and asked the guy: 'I've got the pie and pint. What's the friendly word?'

The barman looked around furtively, and then whispered the immortal words:

'*Don't eat the pie.*'

THIS JUST IN ...

As I sat down to write this chapter, I couldn't escape the feeling that there was something special about it that I'd forgotten. Then I remembered. After a lot of thought I have decided to let neither *Hello!* nor *OK!* magazine into my life. Both had bid several million pounds to get behind my scenes – in a rather intimate way – but I cannot be bought, despite the attraction of the proposal that I should allow a photo of myself to be on the front cover, dancing in the Hawaiian surf, clad only in my thong.

Headlines, headlines. Who needs 'em? Particularly in the foodservice business – we get enough as it is. I thought about the changes in this business that we have all witnessed over the past few years, and some of the unlikely headlines we've read. Then, after my eighth espresso, I went slightly mad, and decided to suggest some of the really, *really* unlikely headlines that might appear over the next five years ...

- Woman Actually Admits Responsibility for Spilled Coffee – Mary Jane Becket, a resident of San Diego, was yesterday admitted to hospital for second-degree burns after spilling hot coffee on her lap while leaving a quick-service drive-through. 'It's all my fault,' she told her bewildered lawyer, 'I ordered hot coffee and that's what I got. I really shouldn't have been fiddling with all those packages while driving.'

- Swiss Army Launches Quick-Serve Concept – Following their success with small knives containing corkscrews and watches, the Swiss Army today launched a quick-serve fondue concept. 'With our brand awareness, it's a no-brainer,' says an Army spokesman, 'Although we are having some problems with the drive-through.'

- Pizza Hut Launches New Academic Range – In a surprise move, aimed at attracting mathematics graduates, Pizza Hut launched its new menu range under the name of *Pizza-Pi*. 'On the exciting new menu there will be a wide variety of toppings,' says PH's spokesperson, 'but each pizza will measure exactly 3.142 inches across, hence *Pizza-Pi*. We expect a big penetration in this key market sector.'

- Burger King Coffee Wins Major International Prize – Fighting off fierce competition, Burger King surprised many delegates by winning the coveted Golden Bean award at the International Coffee Convention held in Monte Carlo. The President of the Convention, Monsieur Georges du Pre, praised many attributes of BK coffee, but particularly its flavour-retention once it's been brewed and left standing on the hot plate for thirteen hours.

- Kentucky Fried Chicken Founder Shock – In documents released today by the White House, under the fifty-years security rule, it was astonishingly revealed that Colonel Harlan Sanders, the founder of KFC, was actually a Russian spy, working under the code name 'Bucket'. The information was filed away by the CIA under 'No Harm Done'.

- Starbucks' New Flavours – Worried by disappointing food sales, Starbucks today introduced a new range of coffee flavours, intended to help it compete more effectively in the tough quick-serve market. Leading the way will be the *Barbequed Rib Cappuccino*, followed by the *Chicken Nugget Latte*, the *Three-Cheese Pizza Espresso* and the *Polish Sausage Frappuccino*.

- New 'Bubba's' Quick-Serve Concept – In an exciting new development for the industry, the first Bubba's was opened in New York yesterday. Selling *only* Gaelic coffee with added salt, the founders expect to have 200 opened by the end of their first year. 'We only sell the one product because it's perfect for our target market,' explains the company spokesperson. 'Gaelic coffee has fat, sugar, caffeine and alcohol in it. If you add salt it's got the five essential food groups for Bubbas – all in one cup.'

- Burger King CEO Celebrates One Year On the Job – A BK spokesperson refused to confirm this rumour ('We won't push our luck') but industry commentators reckon that the current Burger King chief has hit the almost unheard of one-year mark. 'It must be a mistake,' says a well-known Wall Street analyst. 'All I can think of is that he set off on an introductory tour twelve months ago and hasn't got back yet.'

- Surprising New Pepsi Sponsorship – In a move that amazed the competitive soft drink's market watchers, Pepsi announced it was bringing back Michael Jackson in a massive new sponsorship deal. 'Michael still gets incredible media coverage – for example, he's mentioned on the TV news almost every night,' says a Pepsi spokesperson. 'We can't see how this could possibly go wrong – particularly as we plan to do some promotional links with his sister Janet.'

- Fat Child Our Fault, Say Parents – The parents of four-year-old Billy 'Airship' Ritter, who weighed in at twenty-one stones yesterday, reluctantly admit some responsibility for his condition. 'We tried to be kind, helpful parents,' admits Doris Ritter, Billy's mother. 'We fed him every hour for his first three years with recipes we found in an old book about Elvis. We were worried about him getting tired, so we drove him everywhere outside the house and had a mini motor scooter next to his bed in case he had to go to the toilet in the night. We also had one of those stair-lifts fitted so he wouldn't have to climb those nine difficult stairs to get to his room. Our lawyer thinks we should sue the local fast-food restaurant, but we've talked it over and think some of Billy's problem might – just might – be down to us.'

My final suggestion? Don't believe a word of it. If you did, you should get out more.

48 NOUVELLE QSR

In the late 1970s and '80s, we men were assaulted by an evil force. I refer, of course, to nouvelle cuisine. By my definition at the time, it involved going out for dinner, being presented with a meal that you could actually assemble on a cocktail stick if you were so inclined, and then having to stop by a Burger King on the way home for an emergency Whopper.

I peaked with nouvelle cuisine after a visit to Ascot races in England. I had – as ever – accompanied my losing bets with a few beers and had – as a result – developed the normal male appetite associated with said practices. In short, I could have eaten an elephant between two bread vans. Our hosts, however, had other ideas and took us fine dining. It was one of those places where they bring your meal to the table under a silver plate cover, and then the waiters, at some pre-arranged signal, lift them all up simultaneously. This they did, revealing the contents of my plate to be two haricots and a pork medallion the size of my little finger nail. I'm afraid I went down in the history of that restaurant by calling the waiter back and asking if my food had accidentally stuck to the lid he'd taken away. I was not invited back and have avoided nouvelle cuisine ever since.

Two things brought that adventure back to my mental front-burner. I read yet another book on '*Fat America*' – one of about a hundred big sellers on the subject doing the rounds now. Quick-serve, or at least the Big Boys in quick-serve, came out of it badly. My position on the subject remains the same: I am not interested in innocence or guilt, but the quick-service industry is a huge feeder of the world and has both a vested interest *and* a responsibility to contribute to a healthier future. I then found an essay on nouvelle cuisine. It was written in 1973 by Henri Gault and Christian Millau, essentially two travel writers. They noted how a new generation of French chefs was rebelling against the classic excesses of the traditional, rich cuisine of the *Escoffier* heritage. They noted ten things that were happening. I've listed them in *very* summarised form below. Don't read them and think of French food – read them as a list of principles followed by these rebellious chefs that led a revolution:

1. Reduced cooking time (like the Chinese).
2. New uses of products. A lot of traditional foods had eroded in quality as a result of mass production (e.g. chicken), but new ones were available (oysters, asparagus, etc.).
3. Reduced choices on the menu.
4. Awareness of danger (e.g. with fish and crustaceans).
5. Use of modern techniques and technology.
6. Use of fresh ingredients, preferably bought the same day.
7. Avoidance of rich, heavy, pretentious sauces.
8. Do not ignore dieting.
9. Avoidance of gaudy presentation.
10. Invention.

[Author's note: This essay is included in full in Mark Kurlansky's marvellous book *Choice Cuts – a Miscellany of Food Writing*, Vintage Books, 2004.]

When I read the above, it changed my understanding of what nouvelle cuisine was, but it didn't change my (lack of) enthusiasm for the end result. And it did get me thinking about the challenges facing the quick-service business. It could be argued that nothing short of a revolution is needed, and it could be further argued that it is already underway – with some of the big brands making substantial changes in their menu offering.

Can the French Revolution of 1973 offer us some guidelines and direction? I think so, provided we strip out the raw principles behind it and concentrate on them, rather than get bogged down as to whether you should serve a heavy brown sauce with game or not. Go back and read them again. Mark each principle out of ten for its relevance to the challenge facing quick-service. Almost every one scores well, and (in my book) some score very highly.

One interesting point emerges on portion size. The rebels did not list smaller portions anywhere as an overt goal of nouvelle cuisine, despite the fact that Philistines like me assume that's what it was all about. Smaller portions emerged as a result of following the charter of the revolution, and that surely has lessons for us. I am in the camp that says portion size has raged out of control in the US for a decade now, and it is a trend that has now arrived in the UK via the Gulf Stream. I am, however, also in the camp that says portion size has become clearly equated with value for money. You can't just cut the portion size and offer the same stuff. Something will have to compensate for the perceived reduced value of reduced size. It will have to offer increased value via another element being increased – quality, healthiness, freshness, visual attraction, whatever. The answer might lie in developing a similar list of rebellious principles that we now need to follow. In that way, you start again with a clean sheet of paper, and the portion sizes and value for money equations emerge as a result of the new thinking.

Food for thought, as they say. The only problem with this thesis concerns the integrity of the author – i.e. yours truly. I am in my writing den, and I suspect I am the only writer in history to have authored a piece on nouvelle cuisine accompanied by a bacon sandwich the size of a wheelbarrow.

Do not as I do, do as I say!

BIG EASY LOVIN'

I have travelled all over the world, but have only ever lived in England and America. Despite their differences, the two countries have one thing in common – a lot of the population of all the other countries tend to whinge and whine about them.

For a few years, it bothered me. I would come up with articulate defences against the assorted one-eyed accusations levelled against us, but then I realised I was just wasting my time. So I went back to worrying only about my soccer team. Until last week.

I caught Ray Davies in concert, and I am pleased to report that the old rocker and ex-Kink was in fine form. The concert, however, had been delayed a couple of months because Ray had been shot in the leg while on a trip to the US. In the bar at the interval I overheard some guy ranting on about the downsides of the city where he had received his bullet – New Orleans.

Enough. A man can only take so much. You can knock me down, step on my face/slander my name all over the place/do anythin' that you wanna do, but uh-hu honey lay off my ... favourite US city. Still reeling from Hurricane Katrina, I have no doubts it will rise again to assume its place as a planetary treasure. Unsolicited and unpaid, I offer those who were present in that bar, and readers everywhere, ten reasons to look favourably on N'awlins:

1. Hot rice and beans in the French market. This is served in a little tub, and our (then) twelve-year-old son had 178 portions in three days. As a world-renowned catering expert, I calculate the gross margin on hot rice and beans to be 98%.

2. I had a romantic dinner with my wife in Paul Prudhomme's restaurant. On the drinks menu was something called a *chilli-vodka*. I ordered one. In the darkened dining room, I looked lovingly across the table. I raised my glass and proposed a romantic toast. I sipped my drink. My eardrums punctured eight times, my nose streamed, and my eyeballs melted and trickled down my cheeks.

3. Same thing in Pat O'Brien's, with a Hurricane cocktail. Being from Miami, I had to try one (or a couple). No problem. Then I walked outside into the night air, and an invisible baseball bat hit me across the eyes.

4. On one visit, I went jogging around the area where the new casino had just been built. Fats Domino was starring. I spent the rest of my run trying to work out, if he was as old as I think he was when I first saw him in 1964, how old was he on that very morning. I came up with 184, but I could have been out by five years either way.

5. On another trip, I went to the covered football stadium to see Miami Hurricanes in a Bowl match against (I think) Alabama. I have *never* heard a noise that has equalled that made by the crowd when (unfortunately) Alabama took the field.

6. The city boasts one of the best quick-service dishes on the planet – the Po' Boy sandwich. I had one that had shrimp as its main ingredient, and I managed to eat it.

This I did by unhinging my jaw like a reticulated python, and swallowing it inch by inch – *whole*. It's the only way.

7. Coffee and beignets in the *Café du Monde*, by the river, in the early morning sun. Why isn't there one in every city? Why isn't there one on the banks of the Thames in London?

8. Have you ever had shrimp straight out of the kettle, piping hot, and washed down with ice-cold Jax beer – in the approximate ratio of one beer to one shrimp? No? Try it, but I suggest you use a safety net to start with.

9. You can sit and stare, for hours if you want to, and I have, at Big Muddy (the Mississippi) rolling past. You can ponder where it's been and where it's going. You can reflect on its history. You can wonder at its size and stature. You can contemplate the meaning of life. I don't know of any other river that offers this to someone sitting on a bench.

10. My favourite memory. When I visit anywhere, I like to dig down a bit and find places to eat that are a bit off-centre. I had heard about a restaurant, Dooky Chase's, which had been going since 1941. Our son was (about) twelve at the time, and I called a taxi for the three of us (my wife included) and gave the cabbie the address of the restaurant. Now, I can't fancy this up: the only way you can describe the skin colour of the three of us is white, as in *really, deeply white*. In addition, we were also, I suppose, *really, deeply not poor*. According to the taxi driver, neither of these characteristics would stand us in good stead in the neighbourhood that housed Dooky's, and he was very reluctant to take us there. We insisted, although by the time he finished his health-warning speech, our inner confidence was a degree or two less than that which showed on the sur-

face. Man, are we glad we did. We just had the best of times. We met Dooky's widow, Emily, and cherish the memory of our son and her smiling together. Everybody was just great, and I had some fried chicken that I can close my eyes and still taste. We still use Dooky's recipe book (put together by their daughter, Leah) – and in a cold, wintry England it can transport you to a better place.

I'm not sure my memories will be treated by the Louisiana tourist authorities which much enthusiasm. Having just re-read the list, it has the feel of Osama Bin Laden recommending somewhere for a holiday. But I had to stand tall in defending N'awlins against such an unjust attack, particularly after its recent nightmare. It is not a nice thing to do to shoot a Kink, but – considering all the extenuating circumstances above – the city should plea-bargain for a very light sentence.

After Katrina, it has a tough journey ahead. We should all wish it well.

ISLAND IN THE SUN

I think most adults have three places they could call home. Few people today live in their place of birth, but I suspect they are like me and look back on it (probably through rose-coloured lenses) as 'home'. Then, of course, there is the place that is lived in now. This might be somewhere you love or hate, or anything in between depending on circumstances, but is another 'home'.

There is, I think, a third home – a spiritual one. It might be a place you have visited or just a place you have seen in pictures and/or read about, but it is a place that you just *know* is meant for you and somewhere you could live in peace and happiness. I have one of those. It is the Greek island of Crete. I have never lived there, but I have been many times.

Crete is part of Greece, but my spirit is with the island and not with the nation. Greece has wonderful ancient history, but today the nation state is like most others – ridden with the angst and paranoia of modern democracy. The island, however, is something else.

For a start, it's in the Mediterranean, that glorious pool of water that touches (and reflects) three continents. The flooding of the land basin that formed the Mediterranean is thought by many to have been caused by Noah's flood, and the glories of the ancient history of the three continents somehow echo in the surf.

We landed on Crete nearly twenty-five years ago. I know the date exactly because it was that great moment in the story of a family when the youngest child reaches the age of three and you no longer need to drive around in a truck to carry the associated equipment. Our plan was for the four of us (our two boys were then aged three and eight) to land on the island, with one soft bag each, rent a car, and set off – staying at different (un-booked) places every night. Our tactics for finding places to stay (which remain the same to this day) were never to stop at somewhere on the way in to a new town, but to drive through it and work back. We did this when we hit Chania, out west on the island, and stayed at a tiny place that had five rooms to rent, right on the beach.

The family who owned the rooms consisted of Mama, Papa, and four children (three daughters and a son). We never moved for the rest of our trip, and I have just come off the phone from arranging this year's visit. The logistics remain the same – it is 115 paces from my bed to my spot on the beach, itself about ten paces from the surf. In the intervening quarter century, Papa tragically died in an accident, and last month one of the daughters produced the first grandchild.

They now have twenty rooms, which have appeared in batches over the years. They bought the building next door, and one of the daughters runs a car rental business from it. Their beachside restaurant, still based on Mama's cooking, is simple and stunning.

We have watched Chania grow as a town over the same period, but somehow – like the family business and the local community – it has grown and kept its heritage. Our visit last September coincided with the annual festival celebrating the success and safety of the local fishermen. It involved eating a lot of fresh sardines, drinking a lot of wine, and dancing a lot of dances. One of the family daughters, now a stunning, thoroughly modern, cell phone-clad, zero body fat twenty-something appeared in traditional costume and proudly joined the troupe on the makeshift stage on the beach. There was no embarrassment – it was entirely natural. The old ways and the new somehow go hand in hand on this island. We have watched the small family business grow over the years, overcoming the tragic death of Papa. It became clear to me that, without the benefit of business schooling, Mama and the children obeyed two simple rules that many of us forget in the clutter and competition of modern business. They have particular relevance for the quick-serve business – at all levels. Here they are:

1. Expand at a pace you can digest. This is not – repeat *not* – just about money. It is about operation and execution. Quick-service, at all levels, is now littered with the bleached skeletons of businesses that over-extended themselves to grow in step-functions. If you look below the skin of the current well-documented problems of Krispy Kreme, you find indigestible growth aspirations at the core.

2. Focus your energy on retaining your *existing* customers, and you will not need to spend much energy and money chasing new ones. When we got back from last year's visit, we couldn't get over the combination we had just experienced – the family, the beach, the price, the food, the weather, the town – and yapped about it a bit too much in the pub. The result? Six more of our friends are going next year. It is such a powerful message, but so often ignored or forgotten: We exist on a planet that swarms with ho-hum products and services. If you deliver something memorable, you are *distinct*.

If you do achieve this, then word of mouth will get you new business.

Look, not everything is wonderful on Crete. There are too many top-heavy German ladies who insist on going top-less, and these are sights that an impressionable Englishman should not be exposed to. Nor should Crete intrude on your own dreams of your spiritual home.

But try it sometime. And if you can't make it, chew over Mama's two lessons for today's quick-service from the heartland of ancient civilisation.

51

AT YOUR SERVICE

The relationship between the letters that make up 'QSR' have fascinated, and confused, me for some time. R stands for Restaurant, and I'm happy with that – they are not 'stores'. Q is for Quick, and I understand the importance of that. The S trips me up. I'm never quite sure if it stands for Serve or Service, but I don't believe, whether it's a verb or noun, that it gets the weighted credit it should get in making a winning QSR.

Service, and its possible importance (even in our industry), has been on my mind recently. Out of a bunch of travel reading, I picked up two thoughtful studies on the subject, which should give us all a lot to ponder.

The first put forward the thesis that, with the internet/web revolution now behind us, the last great business breakthrough opportunity will be around mixing product, service and price together in a way that blows the customer away. For sure, this is not a new idea, and it has come and gone as a business fashion many times over the history of commerce – but the difference is that, now, all the cards have been flopped and we have to play the hands we have. It's fifty years since The Guru, Ted Levitt, pointed out that the only purpose of being in business is to secure and retain a customer – an idea whose time has finally come. *There are no more silver bullets.*

A second study I read came at the same subject from a different angle. Imagine a graph with five points on the vertical axis, ranging from the 'completely dissatisfied customer' at the bottom, through the mid-point ('satisfied customer'), to the top point ('completely satisfied'). According to the study, if you want repeat purchases, an unsolicited word-of-mouth reputation and customer loyalty, the first four points on the graph won't get it for you. Nope, that's right, satisfied – or even very satisfied – customers won't deliver those three things. Only those who are completely satisfied will. Now, read those three things again and figure out how much you would pay an agency to deliver those for you. Then face the fact that they can't. You control the customer experience.

I digested these two studies then closed my eyes and thought. I went back as far as I could and tried to remember how many times in the past year I've been 'completely' satisfied. Our family buys a big bunch of products and services in the course of a year, and I ranged over as many as I could remember. Here's the final score: *once.*

We were planning a trip to India and got a heads-up to use an Indian travel agency. *Wow!* The agency finished every e-mail with the mantra: *Long after the price is forgotten, the service will be remembered.* And so it will. Their total customer experience was stunning.

When I was a boy in England, the United States was the accepted role model for service. In 1989, I went to live there and found it wasn't so. It was no better, and no worse, than anywhere else in the world. There was a lot of lip service and a lot of 'Have a nice day', but it was generally all ho-hum stuff.

After five years back in Europe, I recently hit the shores of the US again for a five-week, five-city visit, so I thought

I'd put these two theses to the test. Car rental, hotel rooms, quick- and slow-service restaurant food and a whole range of other products and services – all were acquired during the stay. I was ready, even keen, to be completely satisfied by somebody, somewhere. It was a thorough test, conducted under rigorous trial conditions, and I have listed the complex empirical results in the following long and complicated format:

- Number of times 'completely' satisfied: *None.*

This is not to say I wasn't occasionally overwhelmed. When we hit Maryland, I was told I absolutely must have the lump crab cakes at a specific restaurant, so we went to the place and I ordered them. I don't know what I was expecting, but two soccer ball-size creations arrived, each containing the equivalent of Europe's annual output of crab. I set off gamely. After twenty minutes, I was convinced there was more on my plate than when I started. I think they were breeding. I fought my way through one, but then I had to wave my white napkin in surrender. At this point our waitress asked me if I would like to take the other one home. I explained that I was from Planet Europe, where we go out to eat a meal, not adopt it.

Big is not necessarily good. Neither is quick on its own. Only good is good, and only completely is completely.

Here's a poser for you: ask yourself when you were last 'completely' satisfied by any product or service you bought. See? It's hard.

But if you or your company could figure out some way to deliver a completely satisfying experience, the rewards would be such that no paid agency, discounting programme or new product could deliver them. So, pause for a minute and figure out what you could do to hit that jackpot with your operation.

I must go now. I'm going to take my lump crab cake for a walk. We brought him home, and we've christened him Jack. I'm sure we'll learn to love him.

OOPS! SORRY ...

As you know, there are fundamental laws governing the universe. One of them, The Law of Unintended Consequences, is having a bigger and bigger effect on our lives. This law states that while many acts are committed with good intentions, those same acts can often result in unforeseen consequences that threaten to drown any positives.

This Law has been a big factor in my life. Here's an example. My dad was a delightful man. Although we lived in a soccer-mad area of England, he was not a big fan. Still, he decided, one day, when I was about seven years old, to take me to see one of our two local clubs. I do not know why he decided to take me to watch Manchester City rather than Manchester United, but that act of paternal affection condemned me to a lifetime of tears and misery.

The incomparable Barbara Tuchman studied The Law of Unintended Consequences in her *March of Folly* (Ballantine Books, 1984). She actually tried to define the planet's biggest-ever mistake, classifying them by the sheer weight of their unintended consequences. For the record, she came up with the decision, taken by the German High Command, to resume U-boat activity in the Atlantic in 1916. It had been halted after the sinking of the *Lusitania,* and its re-start effectively triggered America's entry into the First World War. The result was a victory for the Allies instead of an exhausted peace. However, it doesn't end there. That single decision brought defeat for Germany – but also reparations, war guilt, Hitler and the Second World War. Let's be honest, that's some mistake.

The Law of Unintended Consequences is in full flow today.

The internet has revolutionised our lives with many positives. It has also, however, provided undreamed-of opportunities for sexual predators, bomb makers, terrorists, identity thieves and copyright violators. Did Al Gore think about all those when he famously invented it?

The Law has also been at work in the quick-serve business, directly and indirectly. Consider the following developments:

- The general move toward using fructose corn syrup as a sweetener, particularly in drinks.
- The increasing mental correlation of food portion size with value.
- The restructuring of the traditional family: more single parents and/or more working mums = reduced home cooking and at-home meals.
- The emancipation of children.
- Cuts in school funding.

Each occurred over the past twenty years, and though there was no master plan, they are all related to one unintended collective consequence – the rise of obesity among children. Again, there's no single big villain at work here. Many of these developments happened in pursuit of the perceived interests of taxpayers, stockholders, customers, families and communities.

Forget obesity for a minute. According to the (US) Centers for Disease Control and Prevention (quoted in Greg Critser's book *Fat Land*), of all babies born in the United States in 2000, one-third will become diabetic at some stage in their lives unless some or all of the unforeseen costs of the aforementioned developments are addressed. In the above sentence, you can probably substitute the UK for the US without changing the figures by much.

Let's not fancy it up: quick-service played a part – albeit by no means the dominating part that many would have us believe – in creating these unintended consequences. It can, and should, play a part in creating some intended solutions.

My point here, however, is rather more mundane than what caused mass-obesity and a type 2 diabetes epidemic. I want you to focus on the idea that any decision has the ability to create unintended consequences.

When you take a decision that affects the future of your business, at whatever level you operate, there is a tendency to focus on the known and positive consequences. If you do X, you are pretty sure Y will happen. Sure, you will probably factor in a pessimistic option, the consequences of it not going quite right. What you won't factor in are the possibilities that the ripple-effects of your decision will trigger something completely unintended simply because you don't, by definition, know what they possibly could be. My advice is to spend a bit of time, just a bit, on some wild, off-the-wall thinking about what just might happen consequently. It could pay back in spades.

I am smiling now. My two grown sons have just popped around. They are also Manchester City fans, and we have just lost – again. For some reason, they are so, so angry with me.

EVER SINCE I COULD TALK ...

So there I was, in the Air France lounge at Mumbai Airport, waiting for a delayed flight, as you do. I wandered over to the magazine rack and there was a copy of *Fortune*. On the front cover was a list of business 'Celebs', and the headline referred to an article inside in which these Warren Buffett 'wannabes' were to tell us what advice had influenced them most in their lives and careers. Thinking that would pass half an hour, I filled up with coffee, grabbed the magazine and headed for a chair – only to find that somebody had ripped the article out completely.

I never did find a full copy, but I spent the rest of the time waiting for my plane reflecting on my version of the article, on what seminal advice I had received over the years. Here's the list, straight from the Air France napkin:

- My dad was hugely influential in shaping my approach to life – but in ways he wouldn't recognise. He had a horrendous decade in the 1940s – being whisked away to war just weeks after he married, and then being captured by the Japanese (with all that entailed). He survived that, returned and I was born, but then my mum died. As he rebuilt his life, I learned from him *not to look backwards*. Indeed, I had my rear-view mirrors surgically removed when I was eighteen. History fascinates me, but I have found that any substantive and/or objective analysis of the 'good ol' days' usually reveals them to be anything but.

- Number two came from the same source. My dad had every reason to feel sorry for himself – *but never did*. I have heard it said that they whom the gods wish to destroy, they first make angry, but that is not so in my book. A good temper is a healthy thing. But I have witnessed self-pity destroy good people. It can be cancerous.

- When James Taylor was awarded an honorary degree at some university, his acceptance speech was beautiful: 'Rehearse every day, and don't do drugs.' With that, he walked off. It was obviously pertinent and personal to him, but it reminded me of Tom Peters: 'If you got more than one priority, you got none.' *The most complex challenges sometimes can – and should – be boiled right down to a few mission-critical priorities.*

- Charles Handy's thinking on modern life structure had a big influence on me. His idea that the three-part life structure (dependence, occupation, dependence) had changed into a four-part script (dependence, occupation, *something else*, dependence) shook me up. His premise is that many people either choose, or are forced (e.g. by losing their life job) to *find something else to do well before the accepted age of retirement*. At forty-eight years old, when I read this, I had known nothing but big business, so I chose to do something completely different. After twelve years of doing it, my wife's still trying to figure out what *it* is.

- Many years ago, working for Shell, I was having a performance review. My boss was a wizened old Scotsman. He rambled on, and I was becoming seriously bored, when he stopped and said, 'I'm only appraising 75% of you. There's a quarter of you that is dark, and I don't want to go in there. It's where your best stuff and your worst stuff comes from, and it's best left alone.' Wow. Ever since that day, *I have had faith in my dark quarter*, although it has landed me into the soup on occasion. I have also never appraised anybody or been appraised without remembering this guy doing his Braveheart impression.

- Hiring people. There are millions of books on this subject, and if there's one thing you *must* get right to lead a business, it's this. Allen Sheppard, my old boss at GrandMet, the company that acquired Burger King, gave me the best, shortest and clearest advice possible on this subject. *Never employ anybody who is not capable of hitting you.* I have nothing to add. You can't improve on the best.

- When I first joined GrandMet, I came in over the head of a veteran. Consequently, he had every reason to want me to fail. He acted in quite the opposite manner and gave me a piece of advice I wish I'd had years earlier. When you are going into a new business, if you really want to understand it, *sign every cheque and initial every bank deposit for a month*. Understand the flows of cash. Whatever the size of business, I could pass on no finer advice. In fact, if I had my way, we would abandon GAAP and all these dubious restructuring charges, extra-ordinary items, and Enron-style, off-balance sheet drivel and concentrate on cash-accounting.

- One last one, and it's to do with writing. We all need to do it, and a lot of us do it badly. If you want to improve your style, let me pass on the advice of Ernest Hemingway, who echoed Winston Churchill. *Write short sentences in short paragraphs*. Then, when you've finished, go back through it and *rake out **all** the adverbs*. I've written six books, and it is advice that has proved gloriously helpful (but I'm weak on the adverbs – see 'gloriously').

These have been my guiding lights. Reading through, however, I realise that there is nothing there for our younger readers, so here's a piece of advice just for you. If you are less than ten years old, and you have a favourite uncle who is always joking, if he points his index finger at you, never, *never*, **never** pull on it.

For the rest of you, feel free to tear this out and steal it. If that's good enough for Warren Buffett, it's good enough for me.

54 INDIA ON 10,000 CALORIES A DAY

Way back in the 1930s, my father served in the British army in India – in the last full decade of the Raj. After a lifetime of hearing and reading about the sub-continent, I'd promised myself a visit, but only when I would have the time and resources to do it properly. That time arrived recently.

They say that when you visit India, you will be changed. You will, trust me. A team of specialist doctors has advised me that I will (hopefully) regain control of my lower bowel within a few months. Yes, if you are there for any length of time, you will probably get a tummy bug, but it's worth it.

First, I will attempt a potted history of the place. Originally mostly Hindu, it has been invaded by two religions. Muslims came nearly 1,000 years ago, and Christianity arrived on the back of British imperialism about 300 years ago. Interestingly, in my view, the British then invented modern franchising by dishing out large globs of the country to friendly princes.

In an attempt to avoid a religious civil war straight after independence, the British partitioned the country, shoving most of the Muslim population into Pakistan and Bangladesh. This action neatly created the bloodbath it was trying to avoid. India's independence finally came in 1947. The planet's biggest democracy was then stifled for more than forty years by the dynastic Nehru–Gandhi governments, which were attracted more to the centralist-socialism of Stalin rather than the enterprise-capitalism that served the other Asian Tigers' economies so well. The country is waking up now, on the back of a prospering IT and service sector, although the march of corporate globalism is causing something of a fundamentalist Hindu backlash.

The country has so much to teach us – in terms of both 'what to do' and 'what not to do'. But it is complicated and demands an open mind. Here's an example: I abhor the idea of arranged marriages. One day, while in India, I heard the subject being discussed by an articulate, intelligent Indian woman. She had no time for the Western model of marriage, where – in her view – the choice of partner is mostly left to inexperienced, naive young people. (Note: this almost exactly defines my wife and I when we met forty years ago.) The whole marriage process and ceremony then places the relationship under ridiculous pressure, based on a foundation of unreal expectations of each other and life's realities. (Note: ditto.) A marriage carefully arranged by wise parents, however, does the opposite – the young couple know they have to work at the relationship from the start and that love is earned over time in a real world and is not a start position in a make-believe one. Has this altered my views on the subject? No, I still abhor it – and my wife and I are still together after forty years of the Western model. But I now have an open mind about there being other models that might work for other people in other circumstances.

Seeing and then trying to understand such differences hammers home the fact that I do not have a monopoly on wisdom. When I reflect on my time in business, I realise that too often my mind was open only to the options that were familiar and comfortable. The quick-service business is now mature, with a long history and heritage. It needs to change with a mixture of evolution and revolution – and choices will have to be made. Open your mind. There may be more options than you think.

It should also make you wonder about conquering alien cultures. There are times when a business contemplates acquiring another business, which may make all the financial sense in the world but may involve a post-acquisition clash of cultures. Sometimes, a business may contemplate entering a new market where the financial logic seems sound but where the existing and new market cultures are like oil and water. A visit to India brings home the fact that the intangible cultural barriers are often more of a threat to success than the tangible financial ones. It was, I think, Norman Mailer who said that *you can never conquer a country if you don't understand the music.* I think that's a wonderful maxim to apply when taking your business into a different cultural arena. Either take the time to understand the music, or stay out. There are a billion people in India, and it is a *huge* potential market with its rapidly expanding middle class. But there are times when it's like being on another planet. Don't go there unless you are prepared to spend the time to 'understand the music' or you can hold hands with someone who does. By the way, the same applies if you are contemplating moving from Seattle into New Orleans.

The sub-continent has many more things to teach us, particularly those of us involved in selling food. For example, the variety of breads is astonishing, and in many instances it is used as a utensil – in combination with the right hand only! I am also convinced that vegetables will – must! – play a much bigger part in the future of quick-service, and the Indian diet is full of ways to make them more attractive and tasty. It was, in fact, my love-at-first-sight relationship with black lentil *dal* that led to my downfall. But there seemed to be a million ways to cook and present all their vegetables. The idea of just boiling and/or steaming them, and then sticking them on the side of your plate to bore you to death, just doesn't seem to occur to anybody in India.

My dad was in the Royal Signals Regiment, which today would be called 'Telecoms' or something. I think I found a couple of his wiring jobs in Jaipur. It had his special trademark, with the blue wire attached to the brown wire and the whole lot covered in black tape. I just smiled and downed another Kingfisher beer in his memory. That's another wonderful local product, and I did a lot of them – just to keep cool, you understand. Hence the 10,000 calories a day.

I'M THINKING ...

At long last, I have found a job that will suit my talents. The only drawback is that I have reached the stage in my life where I do not want a job. If this opportunity had been around thirty years ago, I would have been a shoo-in.

I spotted, buried in the dark world of academia and tenures, an advert, placed by a big department of a prominent international university (based in the US), for a 'Leader' for its *'Thinking Center'*. If ever a job was designed for me, this is it. I could think for England.

Of course, you can't just splash about in the shallow end of such a job. You have to take it seriously. The set-up has to be right, and mine is perfect. My home in England has an old stable block, and over the top of the stables (now garages) runs an old hayloft. This is my office, which will now be known as my *Thinking Centre*. You will notice that, in my version, 'centre' is spelled correctly. My TC has two essentials for such cerebral tasking: broadband internet access and a dartboard. In addition, it has two mission-critical accessories: an armchair and an iPod/iTunes combination containing four and a half days of my CD collection.

Right – eyes almost closed. I'm thinking ...

- Bruce Springsteen is mumbling through my speaker system. I have loved the Boss for – what – thirty years! He combines style and substance like no other. He's like Elton John and Bob Dylan rolled into one. I first saw him with the E Street Band a quarter of a century ago, and his concerts are spectacular. But his content has been equally impressive. Now, I'm thinking whether any quick-service brand has *combined* style and substance to such powerful effect for so long? Answer? I think not. Sadly, I'm thinking Burger King never had it, even when I headed the ship (it was all substance then). Similarly, I'm thinking McDonald's is all style. However, Starbucks had both for a while.
- I am not in the camp of those who either totally hate or love George W. Bush and Tony Blair. But if you scored all the developed world's big leaders out of ten for impressiveness, the total score of those two, plus the French, Italian, German and Russian guy, and the guy with the big hair from Japan, would be the lowest *aggregate* in history.
- The greatest single idea in the history of the planet was the revelation that all organisms compete for resources, and those that have some innate advantage will prosper and pass on that advantage to their offspring. Charles Darwin thought that up, reputedly in an armchair similar to mine. He came under fire for this thought then, and he is still doing so, but I'm thinking you can file all alternatives under 'Fiction'. A further thought of mine is that 'intelligent design' is an idea that can be applied to a club sandwich, but not to the origin of species.
- So, what's the equivalent greatest idea in the history of quick-service? I'm thinking we might have to go back to pre-Neolithic times to find the answer, when the first grain paste (flour and water) flatbreads were produced

more than 5,000 years ago. Today's chapattis, tortillas, pizzas, flatbreads and all versions of modern raised breads stem from that very idea. I'm thinking that whoever invented that first flatbread actually cooked two of them and whacked a bit of dinosaur meat in between and invented the first Whopper.

- Quick-service needs a punk rock-type brand. The business needs an *enfant terrible*, something that challenges every received wisdom and that upsets everybody in quick-service who is older than twenty and breaks all the rules.

- The idea of a lifelong career with one organisation is history. Whether you are eighteen or forty-five, get used to it.

- Any job title that includes the words liaison, deputy or coordinate is a non-job and should be phased out at the next reorganisation. If a job exists that contains any two of those words, I'm thinking you should can it tomorrow.

- The tsunami-type force that is attacking quick-service on the back of health, lifestyle and globalism is being met by a counter-tsunami force of people who are fed up with being told how to live their lives. I have enormous faith in ordinary people to force the kind of changes the quick-service industry needs to make over the next decade without massive amounts of blood being spilled.

- I'm thinking that I cannot go through DFW airport security without my shoes and belt on, and then assume the crucifixion position for the metal-detection sweep, without my pants falling down.

- I have figured out why Holland has a low crime rate. I'm thinking that it's because it's flat, and you can see muggers coming *from half a mile away*. You've time for a cappuccino before you run.

Now, I'm thinking that this is in danger of getting out of control. That's the problem with thinking: You start off determined to follow a path (serious quick-service-related thoughts), but before you know it, you are in Holland. Now I'm thinking that the Spanish idea of a siesta is a good thing, partly because some sleepy music has come on my iPod (which I didn't know I had), and partly because I've got a lot more thinking to do tomorrow. I don't want to use it all up now.

YOU NEVER CAN TELL

Y ou are now in for a treat, as I am going to share with
you the Chuck Berry Rules for Quick-Service. They
are not well known, which is partly due to the fact
that I only invented them about half an hour ago.

I can hear some of you commenting, unhelpfully, that
you have never heard of Chuck Berry and, indeed, some of
you (including some CEOs) were not born when the guy
was strutting his stuff. Well, for those folks, Berry is a vintage rock 'n' roller, still performing at the age of (by my calculation) 146. It is generally admitted that he was a seminal
influence on most early rock stars.

My Chuck Berry Rules for Quick-Service started crys-
tallising when I heard a radio show vote one of his songs as
'Best Rock Song Ever'. The particular song was called *You
Never Can Tell*, but it was why it earned the most votes that
fascinated me. Apparently, great songs of any genre grab
you with the first line – and then keep you hooked. In this
case, Berry's intro, 'It was a teenage wedding and the old
folks wished them well', had everything: wham – the picture
and the story right there!

I wasn't sure about the theory, so I tested it with some of
my all-time favourites and found out it held up well. Listen
to the first line of Sarah McLachlan's *Angel* – 'You spend all

your time waiting for that second chance, for the break that will make it OK' – and you are glued in to find out what happens next. Bruce Springsteen's *Blinded by the Light* has an opening riff followed by the Boss yelling 'Madman drummers, bummers, and Indians in the summer with a teenage diplomat'. Ignore that if you can. And how about Tom Waits' *A Little Rain?* It starts out, 'Well, the Ice Man's mule is parked outside the bar'. Every picture tells a story – you can't wait to find out more. (The Ice Man's *mule?!*)

You don't like my favourites? Neither does my wife, but, hey, try it with your own. I think you'll find the First Line Rule holds up just fine. And what's this got to do with quick-service? It's the same principle: just as winning songs grab you with the first line, winning restaurants grab you well before the food reaches you. First impressions are crucial, with research indicating that many customers make their mind up about a place within two seconds of entering it.

Just stop and think about that. What are the first impressions on show when people come into your place(s)? Sure, you've invested in a nice looking interior, and your food and drink offering is well priced and thought through, but how often do you drive into a Burger King and see a sign saying ' OW H R NG' on the outside? It should, of course, say 'NOW HIRING', but three letters have fallen off. You go into a Starbucks and find the tables haven't been cleared. You go into a Macs and a Great American Family has left the floor underneath one of the tables looking like a tsunami has just passed through, and no one has gotten around to clearing it. These are not criticisms of these fine brands, but they are real, recent experiences of mine.

The problem lies not with the brand specification or operations manual but with the location management, which takes a good brand and uses its discretionary abilities to create a negative first impression. In a perfect world, location management would take a good brand as a base and then use its discretionary abilities to add touches that are designed to impress in the crucial first few seconds. When you next walk into your restaurant(s), see how they make out on the first Chuck Berry Rule. Do you grab your customers with the equivalent of a powerful first line?

There's a second Chuck Berry Rule, but it's one he might not be so happy about. Almost every first- and second-generation big name rock star quotes Chuck Berry as a seminal influence. He was acknowledged as a master of his craft, but the records show that he only ever had one Number One hit in the United States. In his golden period, he reeled off dozens of what were to become classics, but none of them sold massively.

Then, many years later, he got a hit with a puerile piece of double-entendre rubbish called *My Ding-a-ling*. For a guy with his song-writing talent, it must have taken about thirty beers, two minutes of time and a really bad temper to write such drivel. No other rock stars went near making a cover version. But guess what – *it went to the top of the charts*. As the man once said, nobody ever went broke underestimating the taste of the public.

This gives rise to the second Chuck Berry Rule for Quick-Service – it's not about making you feel good as a provider of goods and services; it's about getting lots of people to buy them.

You can invent the finest menu item in the world, made with the highest integrity organic ingredients and with a taste that sends you (personally) to heaven. You can market it with the finest words. You can tell people it's good for them. But you *must* remember that the public knows what it wants, and it may well not be to your own personal taste. They will continue to buy and eat the menu equivalent of *My Ding-a-ling*. You might want to check your next new menu item for its Ding-a-ling qualities.

There they are then, the two Chuck Berry Rules for Quick-Service, and I find that, partly by accident, I have invented a whole new genre of academia. As we speak, I am beginning work on the Ozzy Osbourne Rules for Drive-Through.

LAMENT FOR
THE FRYING PAN

People normally leave the comfort of their homes and travel for a reason. Earlier this year, for example, thousands of ordinary, civilised and domesticated folk left their homes in search of remote locations where there was no TV. The reason? A strong rumour that Pink Floyd was getting together again for the Live8 concerts (enough to send anyone heading for the hills).

I, too, set off on a journey, and the thought of those sad, old men boring a whole new generation was only part of the reason. I went on a personal journey to pay homage to one of the most endangered species on Earth – the frying pan.

Our frying pan was an important part of my growing-up process. Please understand that I'm not talking about a modern day frying pan – dishwasher-safe, non-stick and of a size adequate for a two-egg omelette with the yolks removed. I'm talking about a Frying Pan – big enough to double as a bathtub and made of iron that blackened over time. These Frying Pans were the reason your God invented cholesterol-busting Lipitor.

My lifetime favourite belonged to the wife of my sales manager, a Second World War Bomber Command veteran, who reported to me in my first management position. He would have his sales team meetings at his home, and his wife, officially categorised as a Battleaxe Mark I, would feed the whole sales team using only this majestic piece of equipment. In would go a lump of animal fat and, in no time at all, out would come eggs, sausages, black pudding, bacon, tomatoes, mushrooms and fried breads by the metric ton. My mouth is watering at the memory.

Today, fried breakfasts and the necessary utensil have all but disappeared from the landscape. Both were an everyday part of my school years, and I ended them as skinny as a rake and fit as a fiddle. This was largely because I considered any part of the day spent sitting and/or standing still a complete waste of time.

The Health Police have, of course, now banned almost anything fried. Something called 'Modern Life' has also plunged a dagger into the heart of the idea of a family sitting together around a table in the morning eating something prepared from scratch. My views on these developments are twofold. First, anyone who microwaves an egg and/or bacon should be shot. Second, the demise of the frying pan is exactly correlated with the increase in the average size of the population.

There is a *last stand*, though, and it is taking place in Ireland. To most Americans (i.e., those outside Boston, Chicago and New York), Ireland is a mysterious island, somewhere vaguely near England, noted for black beer, miserable songs, Riverdance and something called 'The Troubles'. Let me expand. There are two Irelands, which is basically the cause of 'The Troubles'. The island is divided into two. Since the 1920s, the Republic of Ireland has been an independent country, while a chunk of the north, called Ulster, has remained under British rule. As this is about frying pans, you do not need to know more – other than that this divide has caused bloodshed in the past, but hopefully a charter has been agreed for those on either side to sort out their grievances via the ballot box. The divide is important to this story because it is in the north that the last stand is taking place and that's where I went to find something called the Ulster Fry (pronounced locally as *Olster Fray*).

I heartily recommend this odyssey. Land yourself in Belfast, and head for the coast of County Antrim. Take your time. Follow the magnificent coastline right round through County Derry, making your overnight stops at bed-and-breakfast places. You will gaze at wondrous cliffs and beaches (including the famous Giant's Causeway), and you will meet some absolutely delightful people. We used Alastair Sawday's *Special Places to Stay in Ireland* and met (among others) a New Jersey widow who bought a ruined old house thirteen years ago and converted it into a thriving bed-and-breakfast business and a French author who came to write a book fifteen years ago and bought an old mountain-top farmhouse and who has done the same thing. We met countless locals, and we started every day with an *Olster Fray*.

I set out to find the best. The competition was fierce, but there has to be a winner. Bob Isles has a B&B in Whitepark Bay, on the Antrim coast – a few miles from the world's oldest distillery at Bushmills. It's in the book. His *Olster Fray* was both a culinary triumph and a work of art. I did not see the pan he cooked it in, and I don't want to. In my mind, it had to be the same as the one wielded by my old sales manager's wife, and if it wasn't, I don't want to know. His signature touch was to include a small triangle of potato bread, lightly fried in a bit of local butter. Halfway through her first mouthful, my wife proposed marriage to him.

To my mind, there is a huge quick-service opportunity here. As we fight back against the Health Police and Modern Life, we need places to meet and eat. I am proposing a worldwide chain of *Olster Frays*, with kitchens equipped only with three-foot diameter iron frying pans. The only drinks available will be Bushmills whiskey and buttermilk, or a combination thereof.

Next to the cooking range will be two pieces of additional, essential equipment – a fire extinguisher and a defibrillator.

UNACCUSTOMED AS I AM …

N ot too long ago, armed only with a bit of luck and some nifty footwork, you could steer your way through a whole quick-service business lifetime without having to stand up in front of an audience.

Not so today. Almost every quick-service organisation of any size is operating with fewer people, more technology, over wider distances, with flatter reporting structures and (always) with bigger issues. Communicating, externally and internally – via spinning, explaining, informing, motivating, briefing, debating or selling – is an everyday part of business life. There is no escape, either, if you seek the refuge of a small business – there's no point in owning and running the best deli in the neighbourhood unless you can stand up in front of banks and/or investors and get them to back you for a second location and then more.

Hey, it's not just about business. On the social front, the demands have become equally unrelenting. Births, deaths and marriages now come with 200-page operating manuals, with clear-cut delegated speaking responsibilities. Many such events are now accompanied by the appalling idea of an 'open microphone', and don't you just squirm when Uncle Harry puts his tumbler of Jameson down and staggers towards the podium? The good news is that you are thinking of getting up next.

Professional public speaking has been a part of my life for a dozen years. I have spoken in nearly as many countries as Condoleezza Rice. I have addressed live audiences ranging in number from an intimate six in Dublin to a raucous 15,000 in Los Angeles. All these experiences have resulted in two beliefs. The first should surprise no one – the general standard of speaking in public is lousy. The second might surprise many – you can improve your public speaking skills significantly and quickly.

Using my own experiences, I started listing my ideas on what works well and, importantly, what doesn't. So, if you've got to address a regional managers' conference next week, or you've got a date with the bank to go through your business plan and your sphincter is clicking away like a Geiger counter at the thought, here are four things you could learn from my hard-earned experience:

1. Treat any lectern as an enemy. Most speakers are directed towards a lectern of some kind, and many treat it as a friend. They cope with early-speech nerves by gripping the sides with both hands. As a result, many an audience has been entertained by the sight (and magnified sound) of a lectern shaking. There's more bad news: This gripping action also solves the infrequent speaker's perpetual dilemma – what *do* you do with your hands and arms? Now, guess what – you can deliver a whole speech without any body or any arm gestures to entertain, emphasise or liven it up. Trust me, this is not the way to an audience's heart. Get out from behind the lectern.

2. Use notes as a prompt, not a script. Don't take sheets of paper up with you; you'll constantly be losing your place, and the temptation will be to read chunks of it. If

you do this, you instantly become a Johnny-One-Note, and your eyes point downwards instead of towards your listeners. I couldn't invent two more effective ways to lose an audience's attention. Your notes should be brutally short words or phrases that trigger the next bit of your speech – which you should then be able to give without further reference, or you shouldn't be doing it. These notes should be in big letters on a piece of card you can hold in one hand (e.g. postcard size). If you need more than one, secure them in the top left corner.

3. Learn to hate slides. If you have a lot of information to impart or points to make, you might feel the need to use a lot of slides. You should fight the urge and minimise their use. In my experience, if a slide is on a screen, the speaker might as well not be there. If you *have* to use some, I suggest you cover the ground in your speech and then stop and summarise the key points on a slide, telling the audience what you are doing. While the slide is up, say nothing – then take it down and carry on, with a dark or blank screen behind you. When you are making slides, remember the T-shirt rule: you can get as much effective information on a slide as you can on the front of a T-shirt. Hand out copies of the complicated stuff afterwards.

4. Remember you have two jobs to do. You might think your role is to inform and/or motivate and/or sell something to an audience. That might be, but you have another, equally important, job, which is to entertain. You will achieve the goals of your speech far more effectively if the audience has enjoyed it. They will remember much more of it if it has been a positive experience for them. For most occasions and for the vast majority of speakers – i.e. those who can't sing or do card tricks or acrobatics – the best way to entertain is to use some

humour. Done carefully and with respect – and with a bit of it pointed at yourself – it's a wonderful catalyst.

If you don't believe me, just think of a couple of much publicised US televised presidential campaign debates. The young can focus on Bill Clinton and Bob Dole in 1996 while the more seasoned readers can remember Kennedy against Nixon in the early 1960s. I doubt anybody can remember the contents of either debate, but two of the four guys hooked up with their audience, and two didn't. Result? Game, set, match and presidencies to Clinton and Kennedy. You might not have as much as a US Presidency to gain in your own speaking challenges, but it's an interesting idea that you could outperform both losers by just following a few basics.

If you want an example of how *not* to do it, just study Gordon Brown, the bookies' favourite to be the UK's next Prime Minister. Look at him gripping a lectern, shuffling wads of paper and giving the appearance that he is chewing a lemon while he is talking down to you.

Just remember some basic dos and don'ts and you are on your way. There's the stage. Off you go. Don't trip over those wires.

59 REM AND CUSTOMER SERVICE

And now, the end is near and I'm finishing up in deep trouble. This despite all the wonderful e-mails I have had over the years, particularly from a bunch of Burger King franchisees who meet regularly to light candles and sacrifice the occasional goat in my memory.

The causes of my current troubles are twofold. A few chapters back, I included a piece I wrote about my 'spiritual home' in a small hotel on a beach in Crete. What I omitted, of course, was the address. I did this so nobody else would find it. On reflection, this seemed to be such selfish behaviour on my part that I have decided to share the secret. The details are at the end.

The second source of my pain was from the same place. When we arrived on the island this year, the family greeted us with their usual warmth – with the exception of the youngest daughter, Maria. I had made the mistake of giving them a copy of what I'd written, which went down very well with all the family, except her. She proceeded to hit me with a *souvlaki* (chunks of tender pork with herbs on a rather sharp skewer). Apparently, in the piece, I had complimented everybody in the place, notably her Mama and older sisters, on their wonderful skills in running everything – and *missed her out completely.* How could I do this (*thump*) when she was not only (*thump*) the best waitress in Crete (*thump*) but also the prettiest in the *whole* of the Mediterranean? **Thump.**

Maria is all of that, and I would add that she has a smile that could light up Denver. But none of those are reasons why she is featured here. She is here because she has another particular skill that is hard to define but so, *so* important in the quick-service industry.

I have found a name for it – and it is that of a famous rock band and a state experienced during sleep. Both are called REM, short for rapid eye movement.

I mean no disrespect to the band, or those sleeping paradoxically, when I steal this title for something I was aware of for years without being able to define it, let alone name it. I have spent a large part of my adult life in the food and drink service industry, and for years I had been aware there was something different about some managers, and some members of staff, that manifested itself when you spoke to them. They would hold a conversation with you without missing a beat, but their eyes seemed to have a life of their own. They never stopped moving – always checking, searching, analysing. Suddenly, the conversation would stop, and they would pounce – and a problem that was about to be born and have a boisterous little life was solved before it saw the light of day.

I called it the REM syndrome, and it has all sorts of versions. I once visited one of Rich Melman's Chicago restaurants with him, and as we went through the door into the main dining room, he paused. He took it all in. After about thirty seconds (count them; it's a long time), he stooped and picked up a tiny bit of paper from under the meet/greet/seat desk and – trust me – those thirty seconds and the pick-up gave a *massive* signal to all management, staff and customers present. If I need to explain what it was, I'm not sure you should be in this the food service business.

Maria has a different version of it. Outside Mama's place there are about thirty tables and probably a hundred covers. Quite frequently, Maria waits on all those tables on her own. In fairness to her American equivalents, she has two factors going for her that would not be present in the US – namely, that people in Mediterranean Europe are never in a mad rush over a meal and that they also tend to prefer cooked food at more ambient temperature – but it is still a phenomenal workload. She manages it, night after night through the summer, armed with that smile and an advanced, untreatable, inoperable case of REM.

Can you teach REM? Can you train your management and staff in it? You can, but it requires some off-road thinking. For starters, it's not really to do with *eyes*; it's much more to do with a *mindset*. It's not what you see; it's how you think. Folk love to try to categorise humans, and I'm no different. To me, there is a *big* difference between those who react and those who try to be proactive. That is not a value judgement; it is just stressing a difference. Folk who react to stuff quickly and positively have great strengths – and sometimes get all the press cover. But those who *anticipate* also have great strengths (i.e. those who are constantly on the alert and see problems just before they surface). If you have one in your camp, you are lucky. Mama is very lucky. Maria is an interplanetary champion.

I hope I can now go back again without being skewered. If you want to pop in, head for Chania in Crete, ask for *Nea Hora* beach, and Mama's is right at the end. It's called *Frini*, and chances are my wife and I will be at the table near the hosepipe. I'll be the one with the *raki* and the piece of cake.

Right, I'm off. Jealous of the success of my fellow authors, particularly the one who wrote the Harry Potter books, I see a movie opportunity for this book – with many potential sequels. I see Brad Pitt playing a (slightly) younger version of my good self.

Have a nice day.

INDEX